Marsha McCloskey's
QUICK CLASSIC QUILTS

Four-Patches to Feathered Stars

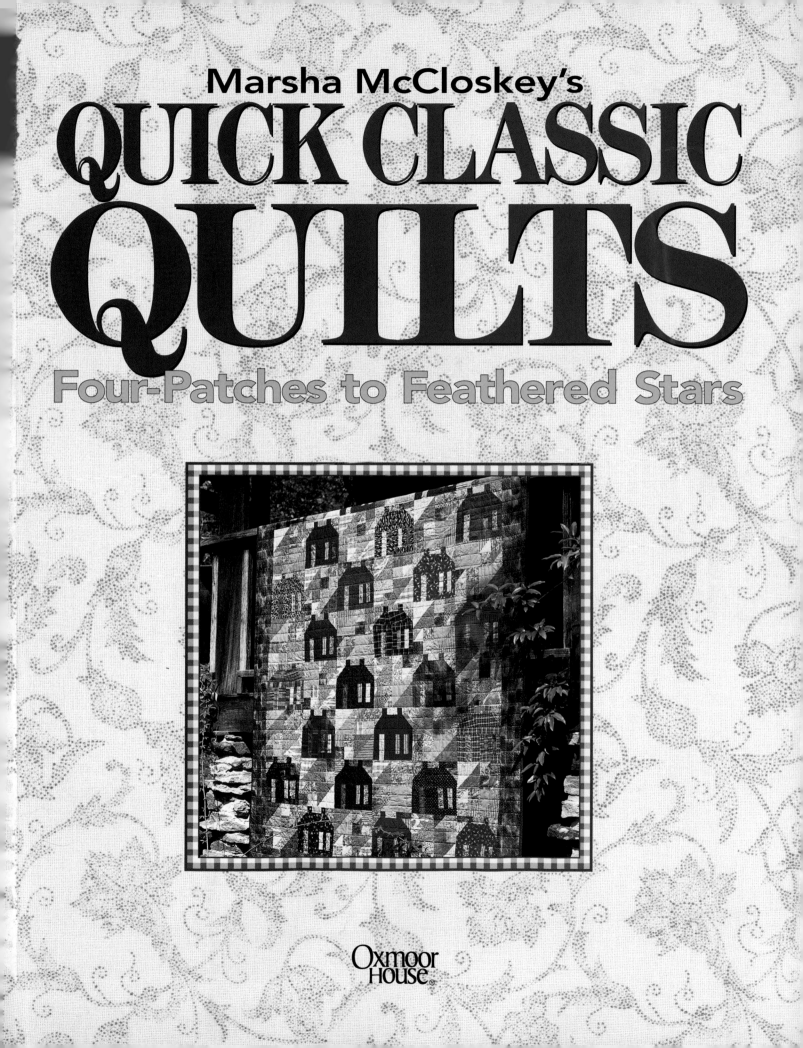

Oxmoor House®

Quick Classic Quilts
from the *For the Love of Quilting* series
©1996 by Marsha McCloskey
Book Division of Southern Progress Corporation
P.O. Box 2463, Birmingham, Alabama 35201

Published by Oxmoor House, Inc., and
Leisure Arts, Inc.

Library of Congress Catalog Card
    Number: 95-72638
Hardcover ISBN: 0-8487-1455-5
Softcover ISBN: 0-8487-1465-2
Manufactured in the United States of America
Second Printing 1996

Editor-in-Chief: Nancy Fitzpatrick Wyatt
Senior Crafts Editor: Susan Ramey Cleveland
Senior Editor, Editorial Services: Olivia K. Wells
Art Director: James Boone

Quick Classic Quilts
Editor: Patricia Wilens
Copy Editor: Susan S. Cheatham
Editorial Assistant: Wendy Wolford Noah
Designer: Emily Albright Parrish
Illustrator: Kelly Davis
Senior Photographer: John O'Hagan
Photo Stylist: Katie Stoddard
Production and Distribution Director: Phillip Lee
Associate Production Managers: Theresa L. Beste,
    Vanessa D. Cobbs
Production Coordinator: Marianne Jordan Wilson
Production Assistant: Valerie Heard

Contents

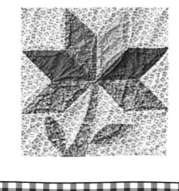

The Classic Quilt Collection

Marsha's fun-to-make quilts appear in order from easiest to most challenging. Select your favorite and follow the detailed instructions.

Master Pattern Section

Glossary of Terms

Acknowledgments, Resources

Tips & Techniques

Introduction

1970s

We make quilts today for reasons that are creative, sentimental, and practical. Like chopping wood, a quilt warms us twice—once with the satisfaction of making it and again when it warms our friends and family.

My first sewing machine was a toy about 8" tall, with a round hand-crank on one end that drove the needle. We have home movies of me one Christmas, cranking that little machine with great concentration, making clothes for the almost anatomically correct Miss Revlon.

My parents gave me a real sewing machine when I went off to college to study graphic arts. Soon, however, marriage and childcare made the messier media impractical. When we moved to New York for my husband's graduate work, we drove cross-country with our daughter, Amanda, and all our belongings— including my sewing machine—in the back seat.

My neighbor in New York was Grace Kastel, who made utility quilts, and I borrowed her cardboard triangle template to make my first quilt. Like Grace, I pieced and quilted on the machine. It never occurred to me that anyone would choose to sew by hand if a machine was available. I could sew and keep track of Amanda, too, and we both liked the arrangement.

I stayed home when Amanda and Matthew were little, making patchwork toys and quilts to sell at craft fairs. Amanda says that, when she was little, the hum of my sewing machine and the clack of Dad's typewriter made her feel secure—she knew exactly where we were and what we were doing.

When the Bicentennial revived interest in quiltmaking, I had learned just enough to be the teacher. I taught quilting for the Seattle store "In the Beginning" and wrote several books on quilt design. In every book and class, I taught machine techniques to make the quilts easy and fast.

The process of making a quilt is as important to me as the finished product. The hours of cutting and sewing, of handling fabric, and enjoying the colors are spent in reverie as I daydream, plan, or listen to music or books on tape. When I sew with friends, talk and stories swirl around us as we work.

I hope you will find that kind of satisfaction making the quilts in this book. They are traditional American

quilts, classic in simplicity and design, favorites for genera-tions past and future.

Marsha McCloskey

My sewing machine is a practical tool of homemaking, and a means of artistic expression and a source of income that leads me to teaching, writing, and traveling around the world.

1980s

Quilter's Primer

Modern tools and techniques make it possible to create traditional-looking quilts in a fraction of the time pioneer quilters spent. Our methods are quick in comparison, but making any quilt, no matter how simple a design, requires a commitment of time and materials. Buying a ready-made bedspread may be faster and even cheaper, but making a quilt invests something of yourself in the process—your creativity, your perspective, and, often, your love. The following pages outline the basic techniques you'll need to make any of the projects in this book.

Fabric and Color

My favorite color and fabric ideas are classic combinations, inspired by old quilts. Many of my quilts are worked in scrap or multi-fabric treatments. Choosing fabrics for your quilt is an important step toward making a successful quilt. And, since quilters are usually fabric lovers, it's fun and exciting to consider all the wonderful possibilities fabrics have to offer.

100% Cotton. For most quilts, the best fabric is a closely woven 100% cotton of broadcloth weight. This light-weight cotton is not sheer or flimsy, nor so heavy that thickness prevents accurate piecing. The thread count, or number of woven threads per inch, is enough to give the fabric body. I like fabric that feels firm and doesn't have too much give. I shouldn't be able to see through it when I hold the fabric up to a light.

Wash First. Wash and color-test fabric before you store it, so that any piece on the shelf is ready to use. Wash lights and darks separately with mild detergent and warm water. If dark fabrics run, rinse these repeatedly in clear water until you see no sign of dye loss. Dry fabric in the dryer and press it before putting it away.

Straight Grain and Bias

Cotton fabric is made of woven threads. Threads that run the length of the fabric, parallel to the selvage, are lengthwise straight grain. Threads that cross the fabric, selvage to selvage, are crosswise straight grain. True bias runs at a 45° angle between straight grains *(Diagram 1)*.

For most patchwork, both straight grains are considered equal. For borders and lattices, it is best to cut on the lengthwise grain because it is the more stable of the two.

Straight grain holds its shape better than bias, so cut pieces should have at least one edge on the straight grain. Plan your cutting so that you get straight grain on the outside edge of pieced units, blocks, set pieces, and pieced borders *(Diagrams 2 and 3)*. In this book, the arrow on each pattern indicates how the piece should be aligned with the straight grain.

The exception to cutting on the straight grain is when you cut a print to use a specific motif or part of the print. If this will cause a bias edge to fall on the outside edge of a block, stabilize the piece with staystitching ⅛" from the bias edge.

Variations on a Theme

If you want to make the quilt exactly the way it looks in the book, just follow the materials list as given. But usually you'll want to create your own color plan.

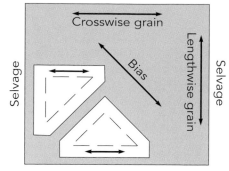

Diagram 1

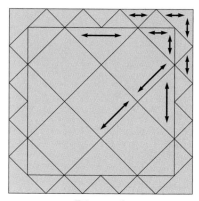

Diagram 2

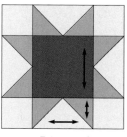

Diagram 3

Begin with a color theme. Your theme may come from another quilt (say, a classic Amish palette), a holiday (pastels for Easter), something from nature (your spring garden), or perhaps the upholstery of your couch.

Color Clues. One fabric can be the inspiration for a whole quilt. This idea print gives you clues as to what other fabrics go with it. Think of related colors and contrasts. If your idea print is dark, choose a light fabric in a related color to go with it.

Consider Contrast. Select fabrics that contrast in color and visual texture to make pieced designs easy to read. Visual texture refers to the look of a print. Is it spotty, smooth, dappled, linear, or swirly? Are the figures large or small, far apart or close together? Too many similar prints create a dull surface or one that is visually confusing. Strive for contrast, mixing large prints with small ones, flowery designs with plaids or stripes. Small, regular prints are calm next to larger, more flamboyant ones.

Another strategy for making your quilt interesting is to vary contrast between blocks. High contrast establishes the design, but the whole quilt is more engaging if some blocks have lower contrast. A good example is *Cleo's Basket* (page 91). That quilt also shows how background fabric is important in creating variation in block contrast. Bright white holds the same design space in blocks as ecru or tan, but a bit of white adds sparkle to the quilt and leads the eye from place to place. Like white, a little yellow is a real eye-catcher, creating movement wherever it appears.

Value Judgments. To choose fabrics and colors for your quilt, study the design and the instructions. The materials list states the color groups needed. Colors may be listed as light or dark, so you'll need to decide what color will be the dark and which the light. Then you can choose supporting colors. For instance, if the list calls for assorted dark blues, you might decide to use dark reds instead. So you'd gather an assortment of red prints, varying intensities and visual textures as much as possible. Perhaps you won't use every piece, but it is important to have as many choices as possible. Do the same with each color or value group in the quilt.

Vary Colors

Resist overmatching. Red fabrics, for example, can range from tomato to maroon to rust to brown but still occupy the same position in the design. As an example, look at the red houses in *Old Maid's Schoolhouse* (page 105). If your colors look boring, throw in a color surprise, such as a true red among subdued shades of cherry and cranberry or a green in a run of blues.

Dare to be Different. Experiment with different prints and color schemes to get just the quilt you want. It's okay to be daring, to break a few rules. Routine choices of color and fabric often result in routine quilts. Don't worry about centering floral motifs—large prints such as cabbage roses really

work best cut randomly. Plaids and stripes can be cut randomly, too, even off-grain. Try using the wrong side of a fabric to get the right tone. If you make a mistake in piecing, leave it in to add interest. If you run out of one fabric, just substitute another and keep going.

Make It Scrappy. Working with many fabrics adds interest to any quilt. When a materials list calls for 1½ yards total assorted fabrics, that means you can choose several prints in the same color range, but the *combined* yardage needed is 1½ yards. You could need more fabric, however, to get the assortment you want. Quilt shops sell fat quarters (18" x 22" pieces), and stocking up on these is an easy way to add variety to your fabric collection.

Set Pieces. The colors of set pieces, alternate blocks, and lattice are an important part of a quilt's design. Set pieces that match the block backgrounds make the patchwork seem to float in a single-color sea (see *Judy's Nine-Patch*, page 46). Contrasting fabric outlines each block and emphasizes its squareness (see *English Wedding Ring*, page 84.

Test Drive. Once you have selected fabrics for your quilt, make a sample block to test your choices. I like to cut pieces for several blocks so I can place them on my design wall to evaluate the effect. This trial run also gives me vital information about block construction and pressing before I cut fabric for the whole quilt.

Rotary Cutting

Most of my quilts are designed for rotary cutting. The following instructions describe rotary cutting for basic shapes: squares, rectangles, triangles, diamonds, octagons, and kites. Patterns on pages 148–157 are for checking rotary-cut pieces, but they are suitable for making templates as well.

Tool Time

Rotary cutters, cutting mats, and cutting rulers come in many sizes and styles *(Photo A)*. Choose tools that feel comfortable and are appropriate to the job at hand. Change the cutter blade often. My favorite cutting mat is 24" x 36" and covers half my work table, but I have a smaller mat for cutting scraps or to carry when I travel.

Rulers. Rotary-cutting rulers are thick, transparent acrylic. Select rulers that are marked in increments of 1", ¼", and ⅛" and have 45°- and 60°-angle lines. The rulers I use most are a 6" x 24" for cutting long strips, a 15" square, and a 3" x 18" or 6" x 12" for small cuts. For cutting two-triangle squares, you'll need a square ruler with a 45°-angle line running corner to corner.

Straight Strips

Straight fabric strips are a mainstay of quiltmaking. Long strips become borders, and shorter ones are used for lattices and in patchwork. Rotary-cut squares and rectangles also begin with fabric strips, which can be cut lengthwise or crosswise. *Cut all strips with the ¼" seam allowance included.*

Fold on Grain. To cut lengthwise strips, fold the fabric on the crosswise grain *(Diagram 1)*. To cut long strips for borders, you may have to fold the fabric several times to get a workable cut. To cut crosswise strips, fold the fabric on the lengthwise grain *(Diagram 2)*. In both cases, place the fabric on the cutting mat with the fold closest to you. When cutting, the bulk of the fabric should be to your right if you are right-handed. Reverse directions if you are left-handed.

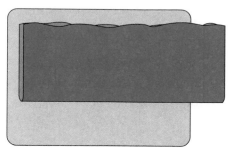

Diagram 1

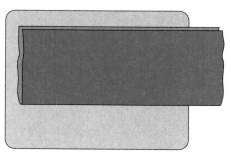

Diagram 2

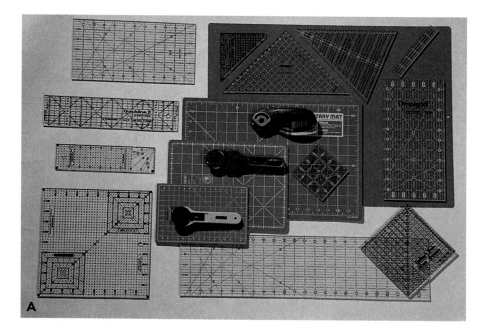

A

Squaring Up. To cut straight strips, you must be sure you're starting with a straight edge. To square up the edge, begin by aligning the bottom edge of a square ruler with the fold; then place a longer ruler to the left of the square *(Photo B)*.

Remove the square, keeping the long ruler firmly in place with your left hand. Place your smallest finger off the left edge of the ruler to serve as an anchor. With the cutter in your right hand, begin rolling the blade on the mat just below the bottom of the fabric. As the blade encounters the fabric, exert firm, even pressure on the cutter as you roll it up the right edge of the ruler *(Photo C)*. Move your left hand along the ruler as you cut, applying pressure to keep the ruler from slipping. Keep your fingers clear of the cutting edge and the rulings accurately positioned on the fabric.

Cut Away. Working in from the trimmed edge, cut strips the desired width *(Photo D)*. Open the strips periodically to make sure your cuts are straight. If strips are not straight, use the square cutting ruler to reestablish a straight edge.

Think about your posture and table height as you cut. Stand comfortably with your body centered on the cutting line (you'll have more control than when sitting). Many quilters are more comfortable if the cutting table is higher than a normal sewing table. Experiment to find the cutting height that is best for you. Some people use a kitchen counter if it is large enough to hold a mat. It often helps to cut at a table that you can walk around to place yourself for efficient cutting without having to move the fabric or the mat.

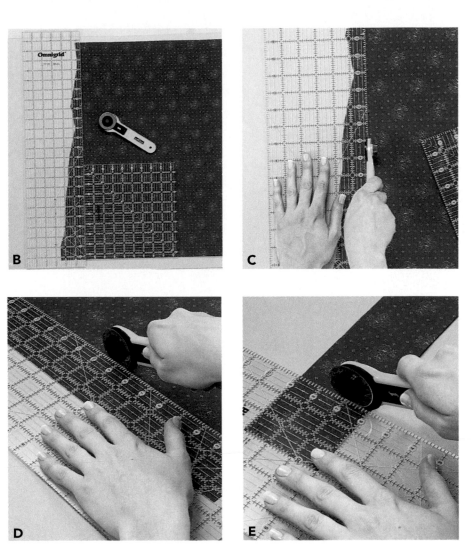

Squares, Rectangles, and Triangles

Check rotary-cut pieces against the patterns in the Master Pattern section (pages 148-157). Each pattern shows the desired finished size inside the seam allowance (broken line). The cut size of the piece is shown inside an icon that also shows the grain line for that piece *(Diagram 3)*.

Start with a Strip. Cut fabric strips that are as wide as the finished size of the square plus seam allowances *(Diagram 3)*. Align the appropriate ruler markings with the top, bottom, and side edges of the strip and cut off a square *(Photo E)*. Cut rectangles from strips in the same manner. *(continued)*

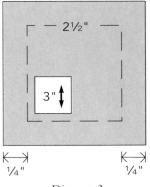

Diagram 3

Triangles from Squares. Cut a square in half diagonally to get two half-square triangles with straight grain on the short legs *(Photo F, left).* Start with a square that is the size of the finished short side of the triangle plus ⅞" *(Diagram 4).* Cut a rectangle in half to get two elongated triangles *(Photo F, right).*

If you need a triangle with the straight grain on the long side (hypotenuse), start with a square that is the size of the finished long edge of the triangle plus 1¼" *(Diagram 5).* In these cases, the instructions direct you to cut the square in quarters diagonally—in other words, cut the square in an X *(Photo F, center).* To do this, make the first diagonal cut; then, without moving the two triangles, realign the ruler and make a diagonal cut in the opposite direction. Check the four quarter-square triangles against the appropriate pattern to be sure they are the correct size.

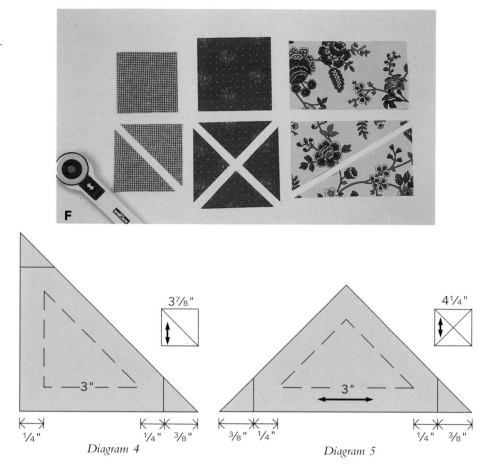

Diagram 4

Diagram 5

Kites

Kites are what I call pieces like the ones in *Radiant Star* because, when I was a kid, kites were shaped like this (see Pattern X2, page 156).

Trim a Triangle. Cut a square the size stated in the instructions; then cut it in half diagonally to get two half-square triangles. Starting on one end of the triangle's long side, measure the same length as the side of the beginning square *(Diagram 6).* Trim the triangle that sticks out. The result is a kite with two long sides equal and two short sides equal.

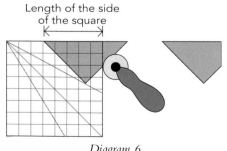

Length of the side
of the square

Diagram 6

Diamonds and Rhomboids

Several quilts in this book are made with diamonds or rhomboids. The 45° diamond is symmetrical—all sides are the same length and opposite angles are equal. A rhomboid is asymmetrical because it has two sides that are slightly longer than the other two sides. Both shapes can be cut from strips. Dimensions for beginning strips are in the cutting instructions for each quilt.

Ace of Diamonds. For 45° diamonds, align the 45°-angle marking on the ruler with the strip end and cut to establish a 45° angle. Align the ruler with the trimmed end to make successive cuts that will yield 45° diamonds *(Photo G).* These cuts are the same width as the original width of the strip *(Diagram 7).*

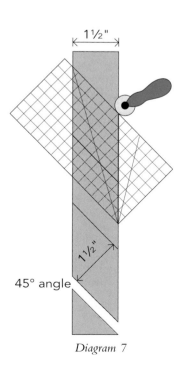

1½"

1½"

45° angle

Diagram 7

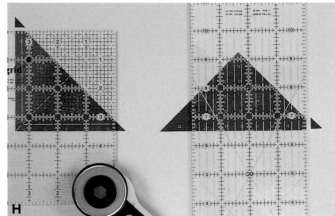

Mirror-image Rhomboids.

Rhomboids are not symmetrical, so it is often necessary to cut reversed, or mirror-imaged, pieces. To cut rhomboids and reversed rhomboids at the same time, start with two strips of fabric defined in the quilt cutting instructions. Place them on a cutting mat with right sides facing. Make a 45°-angle cut at one end of the strips *(Diagram 8)*. Align the ruler with the cut edge to make the next slice, measuring the width stated in the instructions (usually slightly larger than the width of the strip).

Trimming Points for Easy Matching

The extra fabric at the points of triangles and diamonds makes it difficult to correctly match patches for stitching. By trimming points to the ¼" seam allowance, each piece matches its neighbor without guesswork. Trimming points also facilitates accurate stitching. *I don't consider patches ready to sew until the points are trimmed.* Careful quilters trim points from seams before they quilt anyway (to reduce bulk), so it seems sensible to do it before the seams are sewn.

Patterns in this book show trim lines. Points are left on the patterns to aid with checking rotary-cut pieces. Trim cut pieces as described here.

To the Point. For triangles, the angle of the trim depends on how the triangle will be sewn to the adjacent patch. If the triangle's short leg will be sewn to a square, then trim lines are perpendicular to the short leg *(Diagram 9)*. If the triangle's long leg (hypotenuse) is sewn to a square, then the trim lines are perpendicular to the long leg *(Diagram 10)*. Use a ruler to measure the *finished* size of the triangle leg plus ¼" seam allowance on each side. The points of the triangle will stick out ⅜" *(Photo H)*. Trim them off with a rotary cutter.

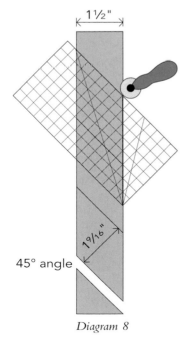

Diagram 8

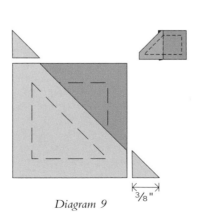

Diagram 9

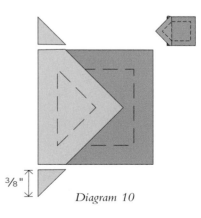

Diagram 10

Machine Piecing

In patchwork, seam allowances are ¼" wide. Maintaining an accurate and consistent ¼" seam is essential. If each seam is off by as little as ¹⁄₁₆", the error multiplies significantly by the time a block is complete.

Measure the Seam. On some sewing machines, you can adjust the needle position to make a ¼" seam. If your needle is not adjustable, use a presser foot that is ¼" from the needle to the outside edge of the foot, providing a consistent guide. These feet are available at sewing supply stores.

Make a Seam Guide. Another way to gauge a seam is to mark the throat plate. To do this, use a sharp pencil with a ruler to draw a line ¼" from the edge of a piece of paper (graph paper works well for this). Lower the machine needle onto the line, drop the foot, and adjust the paper to parallel the foot. Lay masking tape on the throat plate at the edge of the paper. Sew a seam, using the tape as a guide, and check it—if the seam gets wider or narrower, the tape is not straight. Adjust the tape as needed until the seam is accurate.

Accuracy Test. To test your seam allowance, cut three 1½" squares and join them in a row *(Diagram 1)*. Press the seams and measure the resulting strip. If it's not precisely 3½" long, try

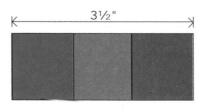

Diagram 1

again with a deeper or shallower seam. Rotary-cut pieces can be slightly smaller than scissor-cut pieces (by two or three threads), and I find they require a scant ¼" seam allowance for the most accurate results.

Getting Started. Set your sewing machine to 12–14 stitches per inch. Use 100% cotton thread in white (or a color as light as the lightest fabric in the project) or a dark neutral thread for piecing dark solids. If your machine's tension is properly adjusted, the thread won't show in the seam. I choose one neutral thread color and use it to sew the whole quilt, regardless of color changes in the fabric. Most often, I use a light thread that won't show through any fabric if the thread is not trimmed completely.

Away You Sew. Sew each seam from cut edge to cut edge of the fabric piece. (The exception is set-in seams, which are described on page 129.) It is not necessary to backtack because most seams will be crossed and held by another. Make it a habit to clip threads as you go. Threads left hanging from the seams can get in the way and be a real nuisance.

To piece a block, join the smallest pieces first to form units. Join smaller units to form larger ones until the block is complete. (See assembly diagrams with quilt instructions.)

Chain Piecing. Chain piecing saves time and thread. To chain-piece, line up several units to be sewn. Sew the first unit as usual, but at the end of the seam do not backtack, clip the thread, or lift the presser foot. Instead, feed in the next unit right on the heels of the first. There will be a little twist of thread between the units *(Photo A)*. Sew all the seams you can at one time. Keep the chain intact to carry it to the ironing board and clip the threads as you press.

X Marks the Point. When triangles are pieced with other units, the seams cross in an X on the back. If the joining seam goes precisely through the center of the X *(Photo B)*, the triangle will have a nice sharp point on the front.

Pinning

Pinning is necessary only for long seams or where seams must align. I find that I do more pinning while setting a quilt top than I do making blocks. Along a seam line, first pin the match points where seams or points meet. Then pin the rest of the seam, easing if necessary. As you stitch a seam, remove each pin just before the needle reaches it.

Pin Matching. Use pins to match seam lines. With right sides facing, align opposing seams, nesting seam allowances. On the top piece, push a pin through the seam line ¼" from the edge *(Photo C)*. Then push the pin through the bottom seam. Set a pin just before the seam.

Easing Fullness. Sometimes two units that should match are slightly different. When joining such units, pin-match opposing seams. Sew with the shorter piece on top *(Diagram 2)*. As you sew, the feed dogs ease the fullness of the bottom piece. If units are too dissimilar to ease without puckering, check the cut size of the pieces and the seam allowances; then remake the unit that varies most from the desired size. I like to pin and match seams on the ironing board. A shot of steam seems to help the rows fit together.

Pressing

Some quiltmakers press every seam immediately, while others finger-press during sewing and save the iron until the block is complete. I press with an iron at some places and finger-press at others, depending on the situation. Experience will teach you what works best. For patchwork, I use a dry iron that has a shot of steam when needed.

One Side. Press seam allowances to one side, toward the darker fabric if possible, to avoid seam allowances showing through light fabrics *(Photo D)*. It is sometimes desirable to press seam allowances open to distribute bulk, as in the feather rows of feathered stars or the center seams of a LeMoyne star.

Opposing Seam Allowances. Press seam allowances in opposite directions from row to row so they nest

where seams meet *(Diagram 3)*. By off-setting seam allowances at each intersection, you minimize bulky lumps under the patchwork. In quilts with lattices or alternate set squares, this means pressing *away* from the pieced block. When blocks are set side by side, pressing is more complex. Think about how blocks will be joined; then plan a piecing and pressing order to include as many opposing seams as possible.

Don't Overdo It. Too much pressing can stretch and distort fabric, as well as make the fabric shiny where there are bumps. When pressing seam allowances, press from the top first. Press the whole seam—don't leave little pleats at the ends. Where several layers create a bump, press only from the back to avoid making a shiny spot.

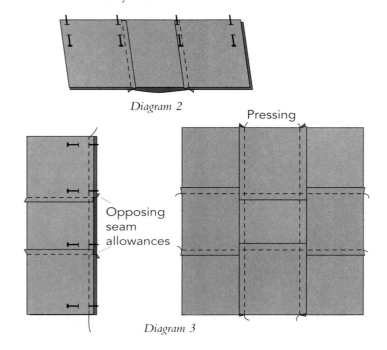

Diagram 2

Diagram 3

Quick-Piecing Techniques

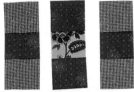

In patchwork, as in all sewing, every edge must be cut and every seam must be sewn. But sometimes we can change the order of these operations to save time or to get more accurate results. In strip piecing, straight-grain or bias strips are cut and joined in multiple-strip units, sometimes called strata or strip sets. Strata are then cut up into small segments, which are joined with others to form a design.

the darker fabric *(Photo B)*, which usually results in opposing seam allowances at points of matching. If the strip colors don't work out that way, press for opposing seams instead of to the dark.

Use a ruler and rotary cutter to measure and make appropriate crosswise cuts to get individual segments *(Photo C)*. Join the cut units to make the desired design *(Photo D)*.

Straight-Strip Piecing

Straight-strip piecing is a great time-saver for checkerboard-type designs like four-patches, nine-patches, and designs like *Burgoyne Surrounded* (page 54), which has repeated units of squares and rectangles.

For straight-strip piecing, cut strips from the *lengthwise grain* of the fabric whenever possible. Lengthwise strips are easier to keep on grain and usually align better with a printed design. Cutting instructions state how wide to cut the strips, which are the finished width *plus* seam allowances. For example, if a finished square will measure 2", you'll cut 2½"-wide strips.

Strips to Blocks. With right sides facing and taking a ¼" seam allowance, join two strips along one long edge *(Photo A)*. Press seam allowances toward

Bias-Strip Piecing for Two-Triangle Squares

Some quilts in this book are made with two-triangle squares. There are several quick methods for making this unit. Bias-strip piecing is my favorite, so my quilt instructions call for this technique. In this method, bias strips are sewn together; then squares are cut from the seams. Because seams are sewn on bias edges, the cut squares are straight-grain on the outer edges.

Start with a Square. To avoid struggling with a lot of yardage, begin by cutting the fabric into manageable pieces. I prefer 8"–15" squares because they fit nicely on a cutting mat. When this technique is used, instructions state the size of the starting squares.

Diagonal Cuts. With right sides facing, place two squares of contrasting fabric on the mat. Cut diagonally from

corner to corner, cutting both layers at the same time *(Photo E)*.

Starting at the cut edge, measure the desired width of the bias strip and cut again *(Photo E)*. The width of the bias strips, specified in project instructions, depends on the desired size of the triangle-square. Continue until the whole square is cut into bias strips.

Stitching a Setup. Pick up one pair of contrasting strips, right sides facing and ready to stitch. Using a ¼" seam allowance, join the strips on the long bias edge. Press seam allowances toward the darker fabric except for two-triangle squares 1¾" or smaller; then press seam allowances open *(Diagram 1)*. Sew and press each pair of strips in the same manner, as well as the two corner triangles. The strip pairs will vary in length *(Photo F)*.

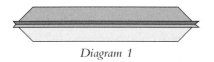

Diagram 1

The most efficient setup for joining strip pairs is a lineup of longest to shortest *(Diagram 2)*. Sew the longest pairs together, then add the next longest, and so on. (You'll have two of each length.) Keep the Vs even at the bottom edge. Corner triangles are joined to each other, but not to the strip setup.

Measure a Square. Use a square ruler with a bias line down its center to measure triangle-squares. Beginning at the bottom right, place the ruler's diagonal line on the first seam line and measure the size of the square with the horizontal and vertical ruler markings. Rotary-cut a square *slightly larger* (up to ⅛") than the desired cut size of the two-triangle unit *(Photo G)*. Two cuts will separate the square from the strips; on each cut, let the cutter go a few threads beyond the seam line to cleanly separate the square from the strips.

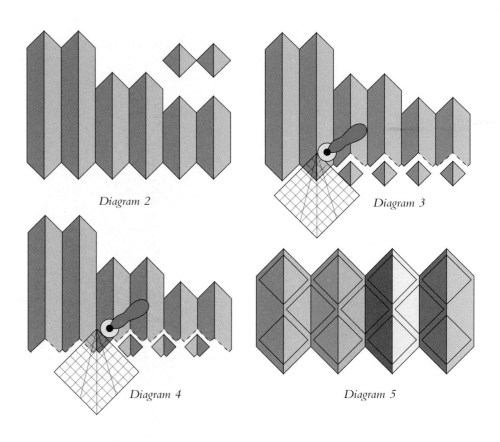

Diagram 2

Diagram 3

Diagram 4

Diagram 5

If your setup has two or more sets of strips, cut squares from alternate seams, working from one side across to the other *(Diagram 3)*. After cutting one row of squares, cut the next row from the skipped seam lines *(Diagram 4)*.

To trim a square to the exact size desired, turn it so the two sides just cut are pointing toward you. Align the ruler's diagonal line with the seam and the appropriate ruler marking with these two sides *(Photo H)*; then make the two final cuts on the remaining sides of the square.

Save leftover strips and triangle-squares for future scrap quilts.

Scrappy Bias Strips. Making two triangle squares from bias strips works well for scrap quilts. Just cut small beginning squares (8" or 9") from a variety of fabrics—the more fabrics, the scrappier your quilt. Cut all the squares into identical bias strips. Before you sew them together, mix and match strips for the maximum variety of combinations. Then cut two-triangle squares in the same manner *(Diagram 5)*.

Setting Blocks Together

A set is the arrangement in which blocks are sewn together. The choice of set is important—the same blocks can look very different in various sets. I usually have a set in mind when I begin a project, but once I've pieced the blocks, I have fun playing with them to find the most interesting set.

It may be wise to put off buying fabric for set pieces or lattices until you've made some of the blocks. You can take them to the store and lay them out on bolts of fabric for consideration. With the possibilities in front of you, the best choice often is obvious.

Measure your blocks before cutting set pieces. Set squares and triangles should match the block size, so adjust the cutting instructions as necessary so the pieces will fit.

Straight Sets

When blocks are joined edge to edge, the patchwork interacts to create new designs where the blocks meet, creating visual effects not present in a single block. A design like *Northwind* (page 102) seems complex, but it's only because adjacent blocks are turned to create different combinations of patchwork. But the assembly is the same

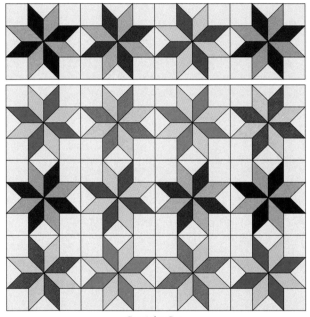

Straight Set

Alternate Straight Set

Diagonal Set

Lattice Set

as for the simpler *Little Cedar Tree* (page 68), edge to edge.

To assemble a straight set, sew blocks together in rows, either horizontally or vertically, as specified in the instructions; then join the rows. Matching seam lines is important to get the best effect.

Alternate Straight Set. In some straight sets, two blocks alternate across the rows, checkerboard style. A good example is *Old Maid's Schoolhouse* (page 105). Sometimes the alternate block is a plain square of fabric, such as in *Judy's Nine-Patch* (page 46).

Lattice Set. Lattice strips separate and define blocks. A lattice set often uses contrasting squares at the intersections where blocks meet. These are called cornerstones. An example is *Prairie Queen* on page 72.

Diagonal Set

In diagonal sets, blocks and set pieces are joined in diagonal rows of different lengths. A diagonal set can be block to block, but in this book diagonal sets are alternating or set with lattice. Examples are *Four-Patch* (page 30) and *Spools & Bobbins* (page 119).

In a diagonal set, triangles fill in the spaces between blocks around the edge of the quilt. These side triangles are cut with the straight grain on the long side that will be along the outside edge of the quilt top.

Joining Blocks

The simplest way to join blocks is in rows, sewing them together in a straight line. The quilts in this book are assembled in this manner.

To arrange pieces in rows, lay out all the blocks and set pieces on the floor, a bed, or on a design wall. Each quilt in this book has a row diagram to help you position each block. This is play time—moving blocks around to find the best balance of color and value is great fun. Try diagonal and straight sets. Consider appropriate border treatments. Don't start sewing until you're happy with the placement of each block.

Block Size. Before you sew a row, measure each block to make sure it is the proper size. Proper size is the stated finished size of the block, plus ½" for seam allowances.

If your blocks are not proper size, make sure they are at least all the *same* size. If blocks vary too much, it is difficult to sew them together. With experience, you will learn how much variance is workable. I can use blocks that vary as much as ³⁄₁₆". When the variance is more than that, I don't use the faulty blocks. If cutting and sewing are precise, blocks will naturally be the proper size.

Pin and Press. As you join blocks in a row, pin-match adjoining seams. If necessary, re-press a seam to offset seam allowances. If some blocks are larger than others, pinning will help determine where easing is required.

When a row is assembled, press seam allowances between blocks in the same direction *(Diagram 1)*. For the next row, press seam allowances in the opposite direction so that seam allowances will offset when rows are joined.

In an alternate set, straight or diagonal, press seam allowances between blocks toward set squares or triangles *(Diagram 2)*. This creates the least bulk and always results in opposing seam allowances when rows are joined.

In a lattice set, assemble horizontal rows with lattice between blocks; then press the new seam allowances toward the lattice *(Diagram 3)*. If necessary, ease the block to match the length of the lattice strip. Assemble the quilt top with rows of lattice between block rows, always pressing seam allowances toward the lattice strips.

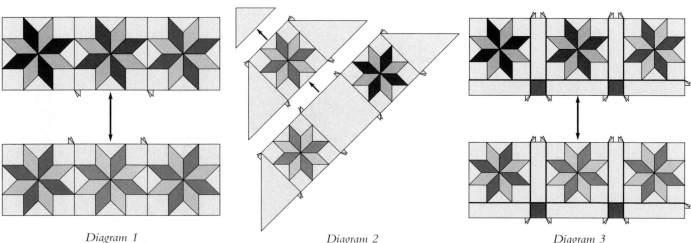

Diagram 1   Diagram 2   Diagram 3

Borders

Most quilts have one or more borders that frame the central design. Borders can be plain with straight corners, plain with mitered corners, multiple plain strips with mitered corners, pieced, or appliquéd.

The colors, shapes, and proportions of border pieces should echo those in the quilt. The color of an outside border makes that color dominant in the quilt. For example, if a quilt has equal amounts of rust, cream, and blue, a blue border emphasizes the blue.

Plain Borders. A plain border is one that is made from a single fabric. If it is cut from a stripe or border print, it can look fancy but still be easy to construct.

It is best to cut plain borders on the lengthwise grain of the fabric. But long, continuous strips require a lot of yardage, which can be costly. I sometimes buy less fabric and seam cross-grain strips to get the needed border length. In these cases, I press the seam allowances open and center the seam on each side for minimum visibility. Because crosswise grain gives, I do this only for inner borders.

Pieced Borders. Pieced borders are usually blocks or portions of blocks joined in rows. Each design unit within a pieced border is called a repeat. A repeat can be simple or complex, square or oblong, pieced or appliquéd, set straight or on the diagonal. In this book, pieced borders are usually saw-tooth (see *Indiana Puzzle,* page 80), so the repeat is a two-triangle square.

For a pieced border to fit, the finished size of the central quilt design must be divisible by the width of the border repeat. If you have a 3" repeat, for example, the space the border is to fit should be divisible by 3".

But the pieced quilt and pieced border rarely measure exactly what they should after all the sewing is done. To get a good fit, I sometimes insert a plain border between the quilt and a pieced border. To determine the width of this spacer strip, I subtract the length of the quilt from the length of the border (*not including seam allowances*) and divide the difference by two. For example, if my border is 60" long and the quilt is 56" long, I need a 2"-wide spacer strip (60" - 56" = 4", 4" ÷ by 2 = 2"). Adding ½" for seam allowances, I cut 2½"-wide strips.

Measuring

It's common for one side of a sewn quilt to be a slightly different measurement than its opposite side. Tiny variables in cutting and piecing just add up. (I once made a quilt with one side 7" longer than the other! Needless to say, nothing would make it lie flat.) In most cases, you can square up the quilt by adding borders of *equal* length.

In this book, cutting instructions for borders include extra length to allow for piecing variations. Before sewing them, it is necessary to measure your quilt to determine how to trim border strips to fit properly. How you measure depends on the type of corner you're making.

Straight Corners. Measure from top to bottom *through the middle* of the quilt, edge to edge (*Diagram 1*). Trim side borders to this length and sew them to the long sides of the quilt. It is often necessary to ease one side of a quilt to fit the border and then have to stretch the opposite side slightly to fit the same border length. In the end, though, both sides are the same.

For top and bottom borders, measure from side to side through the middle of the quilt, including side borders and seam allowances. Trim borders to this length and stitch.

Mitered Corners. First, determine the *finished* outer dimensions of the quilt (*Diagram 2*). Cut borders to this length, adding 3" for seam allowances and ease of matching. Mark the center of each cut border strip.

Next, measure the width and length of the quilt through the center, *not* including seam allowances. Measure the same length on the border strip, working outward from the center, and mark both ends (end point) of the measured length.

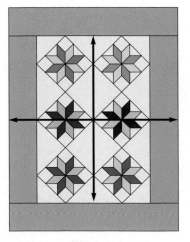

Diagram 1

Diagram 2

Sewing a Mitered Corner

Striped fabrics make lovely borders, but the corners must be mitered to make the fabric motif turn the corner gracefully. It is also important to miter corners of multiple plain borders.

Preparation. Measure and cut border strips as described at left. When using striped fabric, make sure the design is cut the same way for all four borders. Multiple border strips should be sewn together and the resulting striped units treated as a single border for mitering.

Pin the border to the quilt, matching centers and marked end points. Ease and pin everything in between. When pinning borders in place for sewing, I like to pin the quilt to the ironing board to keep it from slipping.

Beginning and ending with a backtack, stitch all four borders to the quilt. Sew from marked end point to end point, leaving ¼" unsewn at each end. Press seam allowances toward the border.

Mark and Sew. With right sides facing, fold the quilt at one corner to align adjacent borders. Pin the quilt center out of the way. Press the borders flat.

Align the 45° angle on your large square ruler with the quilt/border seam line *(Photo A)*. Along the edge of the ruler (which is at a 45° angle to the border), draw a line from the end of the seam allowance to the outside edge of the border. This is the sewing line for the miter. Pin borders together along the sewing line *(Photo B)*.

Beginning with a backstitch at the inside corner, stitch on the drawn line to the outside edge. Check the right side of the quilt to see that the seam lies flat and stripes match up as desired *(Photo C)*. When satisfied with the mitered seam, trim excess fabric to a ¼" seam allowance. Press this seam open *(Photo D)*.

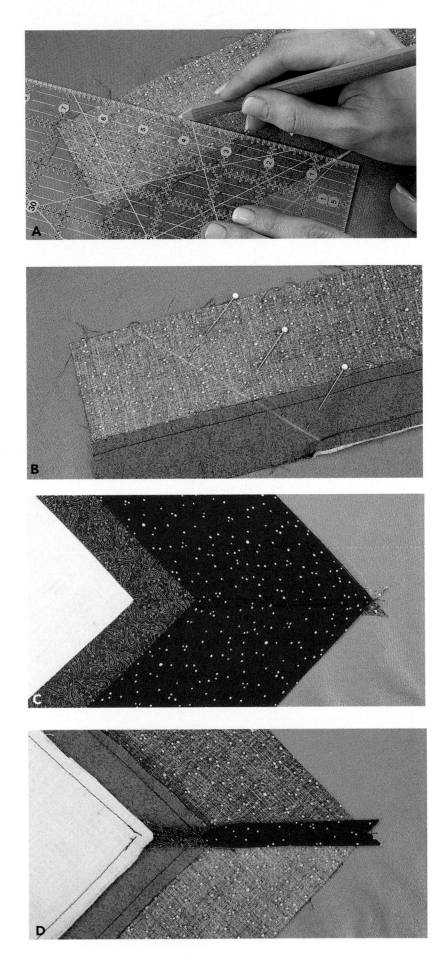

Quilting Designs

Quilting is the process of stitching together the layers of a quilt. But beyond that, quilting embosses the surface of a quilt, giving it beautiful texture. Each line of quilting creates a shadow depression in the surface, so quilted areas recede and unquilted areas stand out or come forward.

There are many traditional quilting styles, some simple and functional, others complex and decorative. I'm a piecer more than a quilter, so my quilting just secures the layers. I enjoy hand quilting, but because I must finish 8–12 quilts a year, I often hire others to quilt for me. So I plan quick, easy quilting that won't cost too much. The quilting must be adequate, but I keep it simple.

The quilting styles that I use most are in-the-ditch, outline quilting, fills, and overall designs. I'll use an occasional motif to fit a specific area of patchwork.

Outline Quilting. Outline quilting is stitched ¼" from the seams, just past the thickness of the seam allowances. Outline quilting doesn't have to be marked, but many quilters use ¼"-wide masking tape as a stitching guide along the seam line. Tape small sections at a time and remove the tape when finished to avoid leaving a sticky residue.

In-the-ditch. The ditch refers to the actual seam. Therefore, quilting in-the-ditch is stitched directly in the seam line, so the quilting nearly disappears. This simple quilting style is ideal for machine quilting.

Straight-line Quilting. Lines of quilting complement patchwork by directing the eye to selected aspects of the design. In *Grandmother's Dream* (page 49), for example, straight diagonal lines of quilting reinforce the illusion of concentric squares.

Outline Quilting

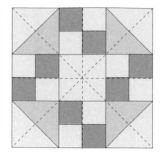
Quilting In-the-Ditch

Straight Line Quilting

Overall Designs. Some quilting designs ignore the natural boundaries of the patchwork and create an allover design. Straight-line overall quilting is easy to mark with a ruler. Curved-line overall designs, such as Baptist Fan and clamshell, require stencils. The fan appears on five quilts in this book: *Four-Patch, Burgoyne Surrounded, Sunshine-in-the-Window Log Cabin, English Wedding Ring,* and *Storm at Sea.* (See the Baptist Fan pattern on the next page.)

Marking

I like to baste the layers together first, and then mark quilting lines with a roll-on chalk marker as I go. However, many quilters mark the quilt top before it is layered and basted. To do this, you need marking pencils, a long ruler or yardstick, stencils for quilting motifs, and a smooth, hard surface on which to work. Press the quilt top thoroughly before you begin.

Test Markers. Before using any marker, test it on fabric scraps to be sure marks will wash out. Don't use just any pencil because that's what your grandmother used. There are several fine-line pencils and chalk markers available that are specially designed to wash out. No matter what marking tool you use, lightly drawn lines are easier to remove than heavy ones.

Stencils. The easiest way to mark a design is to use a stencil. Hundreds of quilting stencils are available at quilt shops and from mail-order sources.

To make your own stencil, trace a design onto freezer paper, template plastic, or peel-and-stick vinyl shelf paper; then use a craft knife to cut little slots along the lines of the design. Place the stencil on the fabric and mark in each slot *(Photo A)*.

A

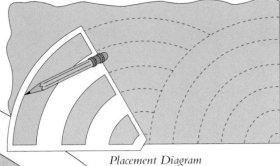

Cut out shaded areas.

Pattern for Baptist Fan Quilting Stencil
To change size of fan, enlarge
or reduce on photocopier as
desired.

Pivot
point

Baptist Fan Quilting

The Baptist Fan is an overall design that's easy to hand-quilt.
To make a stencil, trace the pattern onto template plastic and
cut out the shape with scissors. Use a craft knife or small, sharp
scissors to cut out interior sections. Position the stencil at a
corner to establish the first pivot point (lower right if you are
right-handed, lower left if you are left-handed). Mark the
curves of the cutout sections. Keeping the pivot point in place,
realign the stencil to mark the second half of the fan *(Placement
Diagram)*. Establish the next pivot point at the bottom outside
edge of the first fan. When the first row is marked, move the
stencil to the top of the first arc to mark the next row.

Layering the Quilt

A quilt is a three-layer sandwich held together with quilting stitches. Once your quilt top is complete, it's time to layer it with the batting and backing.

Backing

Each materials list specifies 45"-wide fabric needed for backing. Trim selvages and follow instructions given for assembling the back. Press seam allowances open. For large quilts, you will join two or three lengths of fabric to make a back about 3" larger all around than the quilt top. If you don't want seams in your backing, you can buy 90"-wide or 108"-wide muslin.

Choose a light backing for light-colored quilts. (A dark back can show through to the top). Also, remember that quilting really shows up on a plain fabric. If you don't want to showcase your quilting this way, choose a busy print for the backing as camouflage.

Batting

Precut batting comes in five standard sizes. The precut batt listed for each quilt in this book is the most suitable for the quilt's size. Some stores sell batting by the yard, which might be more practical for your quilt.

Batting comes in several choices of fiber content, loft, softness, and washability. Read the label before selecting batting, particularly for washing guidelines. Spread out the batting for a few hours to let it relax.

Cotton and Polyester. Cotton batting has the flat, thin look of an antique. It is easy to quilt but can be difficult to wash. Bonded polyester batting is easy to stitch and washable. It has more loft than cotton. Avoid bonded batts that feel stiff.

Thick batting is difficult to quilt, but it's nice for a puffy, tied comforter.

A

Layering and Basting

Find a work surface where you can spread out the quilt—a large table, two tables pushed together, or a clean floor.

Lay the backing right side down. Use masking tape to secure the backing to the surface, keeping it flat and wrinkle-free. If the quilt hangs over the sides of the table, start in the quilt center and work in sections.

Lay the batting on top of the backing, centering and smoothing it as you go *(Photo A)*. Trim batting to the size of the backing. Then center the freshly ironed quilt top on the batting, right side up.

Basting. Starting in the center, strategically place a handful of pins to secure the layers, smoothing out fullness to the sides and corners as you go. Take care not to distort the lines of the quilt design and the borders.

Baste with a sewing needle and white thread. Start in the center and baste a line of long stitches to each corner, making a large X *(Diagram 1)*.

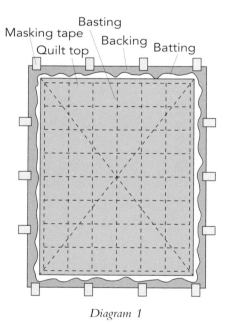

Diagram 1

Then baste a grid of parallel lines 6"–8" apart. Finish with a line of basting ¼" from each edge. Quilts that are quilted with a hoop or on your lap are handled more than those quilted on a frame, so they require more basting. After basting, remove the pins.

Quilting

Your choice of hand or machine quilting depends on the design, intended use of the quilt, and how much time you have. Both can be functional and attractive.

Hand Quilting

To quilt by hand, you need a quilting frame or a hoop, quilting thread, quilting needles, and a thimble. If you're not used to a thimble, you'll find it a must for quilting to prevent the needle from digging into your fingertip.

I use a standing frame. But not everyone has room for such a large, ever-present accessory, nor can it travel with me. I quilt long lines on the frame, but save small, curvy quilting motifs to be quilted in a hoop.

Preparation. Put the basted quilt in a hoop or frame. Start with a size 7 or 8 "between," or quilting needle. (As your skill increases, try a shorter between to make smaller stitches. A higher number indicates a shorter needle.) Thread the needle with 18" of quilting thread and make a small knot in the end.

The Stitch. To quilt, make a small running stitch that goes through all three layers of the quilt. Stitches should be small (8–10 per inch), straight, and evenly spaced. First concentrate on even and straight; tiny comes with practice.

Pop the Knot. To begin, insert the needle through the top about ¾" from the starting point. Pull the needle out where the first stitch will be and tug at the knot until it pops through the top and lodges in the batting *(Diagram 2)*. Make a backstitch and begin quilting.

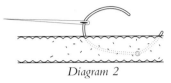

Diagram 2

Rocking the Needle. To make a stitch, insert the needle straight down *(Photo A)*. With your left hand under the quilt, feel for the needle point as it pierces the backing. Roll the needle to a horizontal position, using the underneath hand and the thumb of your sewing hand to pinch the fabric as you push the needle back through the top. Rock the needle back to an upright position to take another stitch. Load 3–4 stitches before pulling the needle through *(Photo B)*. When crossing seams, you might have to "hunt and peck," one stitch at a time.

Ending a Thread. When you have 6" of thread left, make a knot ¼" from the quilt top. Take a backstitch and tug the thread to bury the knot in the batting. Run the thread through the batting and out the top to clip it.

Machine Quilting

I recently purchased a new sewing machine in the hope that it would enable me to machine-quilt some of the many tops I make each year. I read books and took classes, looking for methods that produce quality work but don't take years to perfect. I recommend this to anyone who is serious about machine quilting.

Planning. Choose a small project for your first effort, because the bulk of a large quilt is difficult to manage. Plan simple quilting with continuous straight lines, gentle curves, and few direction changes. Good choices are outline or in-the-ditch quilting, all-over grids, and diagonal lines. Avoid tight, complex designs and don't leave large spaces unquilted.

Preparation. Use an even-feed or walking foot on your machine, and insert a new needle. Set a stitch length of 8–10 stitches per inch. Set your machine to stop with the needle down, or remember to stop sewing with the needle down. Roll the sides of the quilt to the middle and secure the rolls with clips of metal or plastic.

Quilting Lines. Work in long, continuous lines as much as possible. Quilt borders and lattices to secure those areas before you work on smaller sections.

Use your hands to spread the fabric with your hands and maneuver the quilt toward the foot *(Photo C)*. Press the quilt lightly as you complete each section.

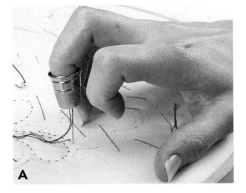

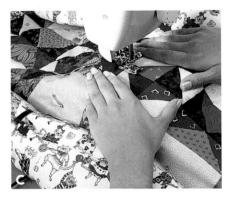

Binding

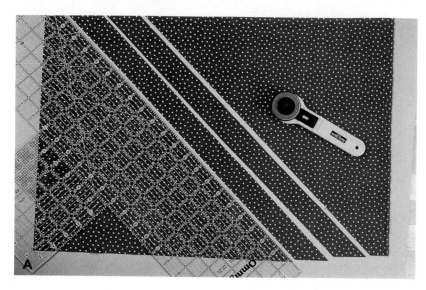

There are several methods for binding the edges of a quilt. The method shown here is my favorite because it makes a binding that is small and flat. Starting with 1½"-wide bias strips, the finished binding is ½" wide.

The size of the fabric piece needed to cut binding strips is specified in the instructions for each quilt.

Making Binding

To find the true bias of the fabric, use two acrylic quilter's rulers—a square with a 45° angle marked down the center and a 24"-long cutting ruler. Align the center diagonal line of the square ruler with the left edge of the fabric to establish a 45° angle; then butt the longer ruler against the square to make the first cut *(Photo A)*.

Measuring outward from the first cut, rotary-cut 1½"-wide bias strips across the width of the fabric. You'll get approximately 5¼ yards of 1½"-wide bias binding from ½ yard of fabric.

End to End. To join the cut strips, match each pair with right sides facing, offsetting the angled ends slightly *(Diagram 1)* and stitch. Trim seam allowance points as needed. Make a continuous strip of binding, long enough to go around your quilt plus a few extra inches. In this book, quilt instructions state the length of the strip needed, including extra. Press seam allowances open.

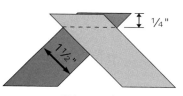

Diagram 1

Applying Binding

Before binding, run a line of basting through all layers close to the edge of the quilt. Trim batting and backing even with the edge of the quilt top. A rotary cutter and long ruler ensure straight edges. Put an even-feed or walking foot on your machine—this helps feed the layers into the machine

evenly, which prevents puckering.

Start at One Side. Aligning raw edges, position one end of the binding strip on the right side of the quilt, in the middle of any side. Leave 2"–3" of binding free before the point where you begin to sew *(Photo B)*. Stitch through all layers with a ¼" seam allowance. Be careful not to stretch the

bias or the quilt edge as you sew.

Stop stitching ¼" from the corner and backtack *(Photo C)*. Placing a pin at this point beforehand will show you where to stop. Clip the threads and remove the quilt from the machine.

Mitered Corners. Fold the binding straight up, away from the corner, and make a 45°-angle fold *(Photo D)*.

Holding this fold in place, fold again, bringing the binding straight down in line with the next edge to be sewn. The top of the second fold should be even with the raw edge of the previously sewn side. Inside this fold is an angled pleat extending from the corner. Begin stitching at the top edge of the quilt, sewing through all layers *(Photo E)*.

Ending. Sew all sides and corners as described, stopping about 4" before the starting point. Backtack and remove the quilt from the machine.

Lap one binding end over the other and press to mark a crease where the ends meet *(Diagram 2)*. With right sides facing, hand-baste a seam along the crease; then check to see that the join lies flat. When satisfied with the seam, stitch it securely either by hand or machine. Trim excess fabric to ¼" and finger-press seam allowances open. Then stitch the unsewn edge of the binding to the quilt.

On the Back. Fold the binding over the edge of the quilt to the back side. Starting at the center of any side, turn the raw edge of the binding under ¼" with the point of the needle as you blindstitch the binding in place on the back. Stitch up to the first corner *(Photo F)*.

At the corner, hold the quilt with the bound edge on the right. Fold the unsewn binding in to form a miter and hold the fold in place with your left thumb. Take one or two stitches in the fold to hold the miter in place; then continue sewing the binding in place on the back of the quilt *(Photo G)*. Stitch all corners in this manner.

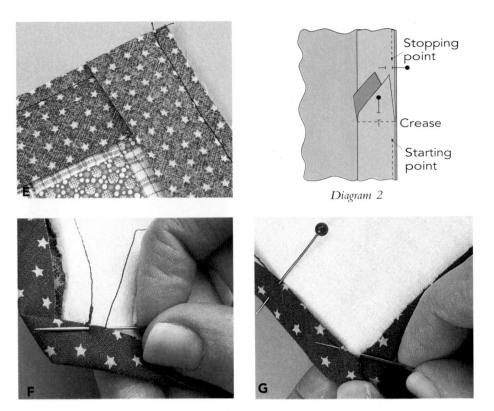

E

Diagram 2

(labels: Stopping point, Crease, Starting point)

F

G

Hanging Sleeve

Hanging a quilt is a great way to display it, but you should protect the quilt by hanging it properly. Nails, staples, and tacks cause tearing and put stress on the fabric. A popular hanging method is to slip a dowel or curtain rod through a sleeve sewn to the backing. This distributes weight and strain evenly across the quilt width.

1. Cut a fabric strip 9" wide and as long as the top edge of the quilt. Piece strips as needed to achieve desired length.

2. On each end of the strip, turn under ½"; then turn under another ½". Topstitch to hem both ends.

3. With wrong sides facing, fold the strip in half lengthwise. Sew the long edges together with a ½" seam allowance, leaving the ends open.

4. Press seam allowances open and to the middle back *(Diagram 1)*, pressing creases at top and bottom. On the back side, press in another crease 1" down from the first crease (shown on diagram in red).

5. With the seam against the backing, center the sleeve just below the binding and pin. Hand-sew sleeve to backing along bottom crease. No stitches should show on the front.

6. Remove pins and fold the top of the sleeve along the second crease. Hand-stitch the second crease in place on the backing *(Diagram 2)*. This allows more fullness to accommodate the bulk of the dowel.

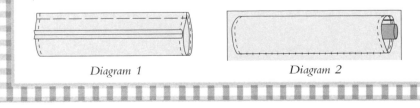

Diagram 1   Diagram 2

The Classic Quilt Collection

I've presented the quilts in this book in order from super-simple Four-Patch designs to more complex Feathered Stars. The easiest, quickest quilts appear first and the hardest at the end, with all degrees of difficulty in between. None require curved seams, but a few have set-in seams or a bit of simple appliqué.

Each set of instructions includes color photos, fabric requirements, step-by-step cutting and sewing instructions, illustrations, and tips on making your quilt a different size.

Full-size patterns for all quilts are in the Master Pattern Section, pages 146–157. Use these patterns to verify the accuracy of your rotary-cut pieces. Or, for traditional scissor cutting, use them to make templates. You'll find general instructions for rotary cutting in the Quilter's Primer on pages 10–13.

Four-Patch

Utility quilts are functional bedcovers, simple designs that you can make quickly and use up with daily wear. These quilts warm us at night, comfort the sick, and support hours of childhood play. Carole Collins, who patterned this quilt after an antique utility quilt, says it was quick, easy, fun to do, and used up lots of scraps.

Four-Patch Block

Materials

	Fabric A (assorted light/medium prints)	1½ yards total
	Fabric B (assorted dark prints)	1½ yards total
	Fabric C (tan homespun check)	4 yards
	Binding fabric (navy)	¾ yard
	Backing fabric	5½ yards
	Precut batting	81" x 96"

* This quilt fits a twin bed. Requirements for other sizes are listed on page 32.

Cutting

Instructions are for rotary cutting. To check cutting accuracy, compare rotary-cut pieces to patterns S7, S13, and T13 (see pattern index, page 146). For traditional piecing, use these patterns to make templates.

From Fabric A (light and medium prints), cut:
• 112 (4") squares (S13), 2 for each block.

From Fabric B (dark prints), cut:
• 112 (4") squares (S13), 2 for each block.

From Fabric C (tan check), cut:
• 4 (4" x 93") lengthwise strips for borders.
• 42 (7½") squares (S7) for alternate set squares.
• 7 (11⅛") squares. Cut each square in quarters diagonally to get 4 triangles from each square, a total of 26 (and 2 extra) quarter-square triangles for side set triangles.
• 2 (5⅞") squares. Cut each square in half diagonally to get 4 corner set triangles (T13).

Making Blocks

1. For 1 Four-Patch, select 2 matching Fabric A squares and 2 matching Fabric B squares.

2. Join each light square to a dark square. Press seam allowances toward dark squares.

3. Join 2 pieced units to complete 1 block *(Block Assembly Diagram)*. Repeat to make a total of 56 blocks.

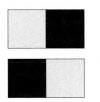

Block Assembly Diagram

Quilt Assembly

To assemble this quilt, set blocks on the diagonal, alternating with square set pieces.

1. Lay out Four-Patch blocks in diagonal rows, alternating blocks with set squares *(Quilt Assembly Diagram)*. Position a set triangle at end of each row as shown.

2. Join blocks and set pieces in diagonal rows as shown. Press seam allowances toward set pieces. Join rows.

(continued)

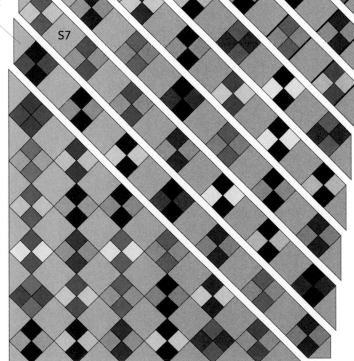

Quilt Assembly Diagram

Adding Border

1. Referring to instructions on page 20, measure quilt from top to bottom; then trim 2 border strips to match length. Join borders to quilt sides. Press seam allowances toward borders.
2. Measure quilt from side to side; then trim remaining borders to match quilt width. Join borders to top and bottom edges. Press seam allowances toward borders.

Finishing

1. Mark quilting design on quilt top as desired. Quilt shown is hand-quilted in a traditional Baptist Fan design. Carole Collins calls this all-over quilting design "Daisy's Fan" after her mother-in-law, who taught Carole to quilt. Years ago, Daisy marked the pattern by tracing around her hand spread in a semi-circle. Pattern and instructions to mark design are on page 23. Two other quilting suggestions are shown here *(Alternate Quilting Diagrams)*.
2. Divide backing fabric into 2 (2¾-yard) lengths. Join lengths to make backing. Layer backing, batting, and quilt top. Baste. Quilt as desired.
3. Cut 9 yards of 1½"-wide bias binding. See page 26 for instructions on making and applying binding.

Size Variations

	Wall/Crib	Full/Queen	King
Finished Size	47½" x 47½"	86" x 96"	96" x 96"
Number of Blocks	16	72	81
Blocks Set	4 x 4	8 x 9	9 x 9
Number of Set Squares	9	56	64
Number of Side Set Triangles	12	30	32

Materials for Size Variations

		Wall/Crib	Full/Queen	King
	Fabric A	½ yard	1¾ yards	2 yards
	Fabric B	½ yard	1¾ yards	2 yards
	Fabric C	1½ yards	4½ yards	4½ yards
	Binding	½ yard	¾ yard	¾ yard
	Backing	2⅞ yards	8½ yards	8½ yards

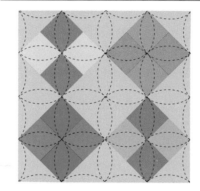 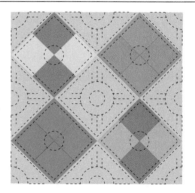

Alternate Quilting Diagrams

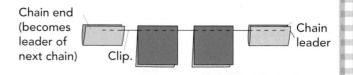

Four-Patch by Carole Collins, Norfolk, Nebraska, 1990.

Sawtooth Star & Four-Patch

The Sawtooth Star is one of the most beloved patterns in patchwork—it has simple shapes and is easy to piece. This small quilt combines two blocks, the star and a Double Four-Patch, to make an overall design that is very satisfying.

Sawtooth Star & Four-Patch by Marsha McCloskey, Seattle, Washington, 1995. Hand-quilted.

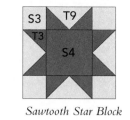

Sawtooth Star Block

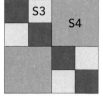

Double Four-Patch
Block 1

Double Four-Patch
Block 2

Approximate finished size: 42" x 54"* • Blocks: 18 (6") Sawtooth Star blocks,
17 (6") Double Four-Patch blocks

Materials

	Fabric A (pink print or scraps)	1⅜ yards
	Fabric B (dark green)	¼ yard
	Fabric C (light green)	¼ yard
	Fabric D (muslin)	¾ yard
	Fabric E (light large floral)	1½ yards
	Fabric F (beige plaid)	⅜ yard
	Binding (green)	½ yard
	Backing fabric	1¾ yards
	Precut batting	45" x 60"

* This quilt is a crib size or wall hanging. Requirements for other sizes are listed on page 37.

Cutting

Instructions are for rotary cutting. To check cutting accuracy, compare rotary-cut pieces to patterns S3, S4, T3, and T9 (see pattern index, page 146). For traditional piecing, use these patterns to make templates.

From Fabric A (pink), cut:
• 4 (1¼" x 46") lengthwise strips for middle border.
• 18 (3½") squares (S4), 1 for each star block.
• 72 (2⅜") squares. Cut each square in half diagonally to get 144 half-square triangles (T3), 8 for each star block.

From Fabric B (dark green), cut:
• 2 (2" x 44") crosswise strips for strip piecing *or* 32 (2") squares (S3), 4 for each of 8 four-patch blocks.

From Fabric C (light green), cut:
• 2 (2" x 44") crosswise strips for strip piecing *or* 36 (2") squares (S3), 4 for each of 9 four-patch blocks.

From Fabric D (muslin), cut:
• 4 (2" x 44") crosswise strips for strip piecing *or* 68 (2") squares (S3), 4 for each four-patch block.
• 72 (2") squares (S3), 4 for each star block.
• 18 (4¼") squares. Cut each square in quarters diagonally to get 72 quarter-square triangles (T9), 4 for each star block.

From Fabric E (large floral), cut:
• 4 (4½" x 50") lengthwise strips for outer border.
• 34 (3½") squares (S4), 2 for each four-patch block.

From Fabric F (beige plaid), cut:
• 4 (2" x 44") crosswise strips for inner border.

Making Star Blocks

1. For 1 star block, select 4 S3 squares and 4 T9 triangles of Fabric D, and 8 T3 triangles and 1 S4 square of Fabric A.

2. For star points, join 2 Fabric A triangles to each Fabric D triangle to make 4 star-point units. Press seam allowances toward Fabric A.

3. Assemble star-point units with squares in 3 rows *(Sawtooth Star Block Assembly Diagram)*. Sew a Fabric D square to each end of 2 star-point units and press seam allowances toward Fabric D. Join remaining star-point units to sides of Fabric A square. Press seam allowances toward square.

4. Join rows to complete block. Repeat to make a total of 18 Sawtooth Star blocks. *(continued)*

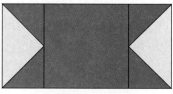

Sawtooth Star Block Assembly Diagram

Making Double Four-Patch Blocks

There are two Double Four-Patch blocks. Both are made the same way, but Block 1 uses Fabric B (dark green) and Block 2 uses Fabric C (light green).

1. Join each strip of Fabric B to 1 Fabric D strip, making 2 strata or strip sets. Press seam allowances toward Fabric B.

2. With right sides facing, match both strip sets so that each fabric faces the other and opposing seam allowances are nested *(Diagram A)*. Rotary-cut 2"-wide segments from nested strips. Cut 16 units from each strip. (If you prefer traditional piecing with individual squares, join squares of fabrics B and D to make 32 segments as shown.)

3. Join each pair of cut units to make 1 four-patch *(Diagram B)*.

4. For each block, select 2 four-patches and 2 Fabric E squares. Join a square to each four-patch *(Double Four-Patch Block Assembly Diagram)*. Press seam allowances toward large squares. Join units to complete Block 1.

5. Repeat to make a total of 8 of Block 1 with Fabric B. In same manner, make 9 of Block 2 with Fabric C.

Quilt Assembly

1. To make Row 1, join 3 star blocks with 2 four-patch blocks *(Quilt Assembly Diagram),* noting placement of light and dark four-patches. Make 2 of Row 1.

2. To make Row 2, join 3 four-patch blocks with 2 star blocks, placing light and dark four-patches as shown. Make 2 of Row 2.

3. Make Row 3 like Row 1, changing placement of light and dark four-patches. Make 2 of Row 3.

4. Make 1 of Row 4 as shown.

5. Join block rows in order shown.

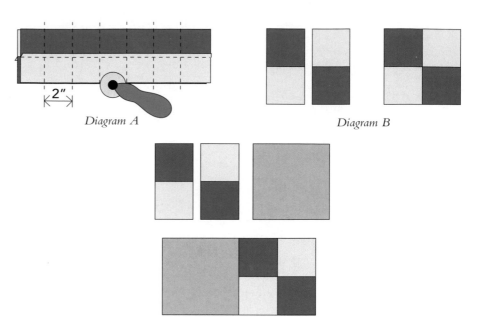

Diagram A

Diagram B

Double Four-Patch Block Assembly Diagram

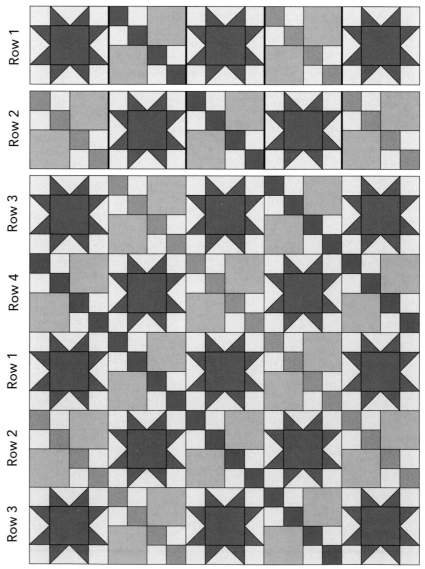

Row 1

Row 2

Row 3

Row 4

Row 1

Row 2

Row 3

Quilt Assembly Diagram

Adding Borders

1. Referring to instructions on page 20, measure quilt from top to bottom and trim 2 strips of Fabric F to match. Join borders to quilt sides. Press seam allowances toward borders.

2. Measure quilt from side to side; then trim remaining Fabric F strips to match width. Join borders to top and bottom edges.

3. Join Fabric A strips to quilt in same manner for middle border.

4. Repeat to join Fabric E outer borders.

Finishing

1. Mark quilting design on quilt top as desired. On quilt shown, stars are outline-quilted and diagonal lines make an X through each Double Four-Patch block, emphasizing continuous chains of same-color four-patches. Two other quilting suggestions are shown here *(Alternate Quilting Diagrams)*.

2. Layer backing, batting, and quilt top. Baste. Quilt as marked or as desired.

3. Cut 5¼ yards of 1½"-wide bias binding. See page 26 for instructions on making and applying binding.

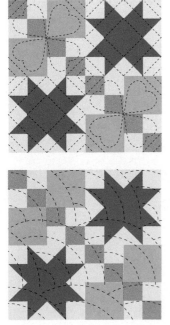

Alternate Quilting Diagrams

Size Variations

	Twin	Full/Queen	King
Finished Size	66" x 90"	90" x 90"	102" x 102"
Blocks Set	9 x 13	13 x 13	15 x 15
Number of Sawtooth Star Blocks	59	85	113
Number of Double Four-Patch Blocks	58	84	112

Materials for Size Variations

		Twin	Full/Queen	King
	Fabric A	2⅜ yards	2⅜ yards	3 yards
	Fabric B	⅜ yard	½ yard	¾ yard
	Fabric C	⅜ yard	½ yard	¾ yard
	Fabric D	2⅛ yards	3 yards	4 yards
	Fabric E	2½ yards	2½ yards	3 yards
	Fabric F*	½ yard	⅝ yard	⅞ yard
	Binding	⅝ yard	¾ yard	¾ yard
	Backing	5⅝ yards	8¼ yards	9 yards

* Cut strips crosswise.

Rotary Cutter Safety

Before you use a rotary cutter for the first time, stop to think about safety. A rotary-cutter blade is so sharp that you can easily cut yourself, other people, or objects that you have no intention of slicing. Here are a few tips to follow when you work with this wonderful tool.

• Keep the safety shield over the blade when not in use.

• Always roll the cutter away from you. Plan your cutting so hands and fingers are not at risk.

• Keep the cutter out of the reach of children.

• Discard a used blade responsibly. Tape cardboard around it before tossing a blade in the trash. Better yet, recycle—resharpening services advertise in quilt magazines. And there are new do-it-yourself sharpening gadgets available that give good results.

Buckeye Beauty

This quilt looks scrappy, but it took planning to get the right effect. Quiltmaker Reynola Pakusich used lots of fabrics in four colors chosen to coordinate with the floral stripe of the middle border. Reynola mixed light neutrals with light, medium, and dark fabrics in blue, gold, brown, and green. If you choose to play with random scraps, be sure to keep value placement consistent.

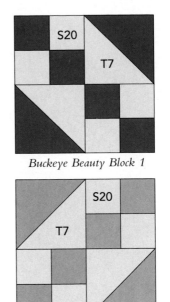

Buckeye Beauty Block 1

Buckeye Beauty Block 2

Materials

■	Fabric A (assorted dark prints)	2¾ yards total
▩	Fabric B (assorted medium prints)	2¾ yards total
□	Fabric C (assorted light prints)	5 yards total
	Fabric D (2 dark solids for inner border)	⅜ yard each
	Fabric E (stripe for middle border)	3⅜ yards
	Fabric F (dark print for outer border)	1⅜ yards
	Binding	1 yard
	Backing fabric	9¼ yards
	Precut batting	120" x 120"

* This quilt fits a king-size bed. Requirements for other sizes are listed on page 40.

Cutting

Instructions are for rotary cutting. To check cutting accuracy, compare rotary-cut pieces to patterns S20 and T7 (see pattern index, page 146.) For traditional piecing, use these patterns to make templates.

You can quick-piece this block, but Reynola cut individual pieces so she could place them by value. She made 2 types of blocks—Block 1 has dark prints mixed with lights, and Block 2 has medium prints mixed with lights. Where alternating blocks meet, medium and dark fabrics make four-patches and four-triangle squares.

From Fabric A (dark prints), cut:
• 66 (4⅞") squares. Cut each square in half diagonally to get 132 triangles (T7), 2 for each Block 1.
• 264 (2½") squares (S20), 4 for each Block 1.

From Fabric B (medium prints), cut:
• 66 (4⅞") squares. Cut each square in half diagonally to get 132 triangles (T7), 2 for each Block 2.
• 264 (2½") squares (S20), 4 for each Block 2.

From Fabric C (light prints), cut:
• 132 (4⅞") squares. Cut each square in half diagonally to get 264 triangles (T7), 2 for each block.
• 528 (2½") squares (S4), 4 for each block.

From Fabric D (2 dark solids), cut:
• 6 (1½" x 44") crosswise strips from *each* fabric for inner border.

From Fabric E (stripe), cut:
• 4 (4¾" x 116") lengthwise strips for middle border.

From Fabric F (dark print), cut:
• 12 (3¾" x 44") crosswise strips for outer border.

Making Blocks

1. For each Block 1, select 4 squares and 2 triangles *each* of fabrics A (dark) and C (light).

2. Join each Fabric A square to 1 Fabric C square *(Diagram A)*. Press seam allowances toward dark square. Join 2 units to make a four-patch as shown. Make 2 four-patches.

3. Join each Fabric A triangle to 1 Fabric C triangle to make 2 two-triangle squares *(Diagram B)*.

4. Join four-patches and two-triangle squares to complete 1 block *(Block Assembly Diagram)*. Repeat to make a total of 66 of Block 1.

5. Make 66 of Block 2 in same manner, using fabrics B (medium) and C (light). *(continued)*

Diagram A

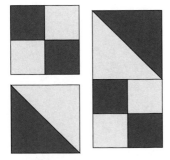

Block Assembly Diagram

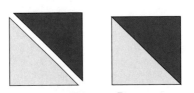

Diagram B

Quilt Assembly

1. To make Row 1, join 6 of Block 1 and 5 of Block 2 *(Row Assembly Diagram)*. Alternate positions of blocks as shown, always sewing triangles to triangles and four-patches to four-patches. Make 6 of Row 1.

2. To make Row 2, join 5 of Block 1 and 6 of Block 2 as shown. Make 6 of Row 2.

3. Starting with Row 1, join rows, alternating rows 1 and 2.

Adding Borders

1. Join strips of Fabric D end-to-end to make 2 (1½" x 116") strips of each fabric. Join strips of Fabric F end-to-end in same manner to make 4 (3¾" x 116") strips.

2. Join 4 sets of border strips, sewing D and F strips to opposite edges of each Fabric E strip to get 4 (9" x 116") border units. Press seam allowances away from center strip. On inside edge (Fabric D), mark center of each unit.

3. Review instructions on pages 20 and 21 for making a mitered corner. Measure quilt from top to bottom and from side to side.

4. Measuring out from center mark, measure length of quilt on 2 border units (1 each of Fabric D). Mark corner end points on border units. Pin borders to quilt sides, matching centers and corners. Sew borders to sides.

5. Measure and mark width of quilt on remaining 2 border units. Pin and sew borders to top and bottom edges of quilt. Press seam allowances toward borders.

6. Miter corners.

Finishing

1. Mark quilting design on quilt top as desired. On quilt shown, straight-line quilting connects chains of four-patches and a tulip motif is quilted over the triangle-squares. Two other quilting suggestions are shown here *(Alternate Quilting Diagrams)*.

2. Divide backing fabric into 3 (3⅛-yard) lengths. Join lengths to make backing.

3. Layer backing, batting, and quilt top. (Backing seams parallel top and bottom edges of quilt top.) Baste. Quilt as marked or as desired.

4. Cut 12 yards of 1½"-wide bias binding. See page 26 for instructions on making and applying binding.

Row Assembly Diagram

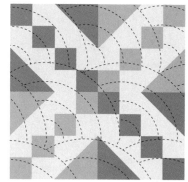 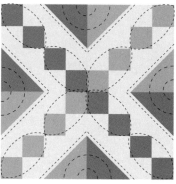

Alternate Quilting Diagrams

Size Variations

	Twin	Full	Queen
Finished Size	65" x 89"	81" x 97"	89" x 97"
Number of Blocks	54	80	90
Blocks Set	6 x 9	8 x 10	9 x 10

Materials for Size Variations

		Twin	Full	Queen
	Fabric A	1 yard	1½ yards	1½ yards
	Fabric B	1 yard	1½ yards	1½ yards
	Fabric C	2 yards	3 yards	3 yards
	Fabric D*	⅜ yard	½ yard	⅝ yard
	Fabric E	2⅝ yards	3 yards	3 yards
	Fabric F*	1 yard	1⅛ yards	1⅜ yards
	Binding	¾ yard	¾ yard	¾ yard
	Backing	5½ yards	6 yards	8¼ yards

* Cut strips crosswise.

Buckeye Beauty by Reynola Pakusich, Bellingham, Washington, 1987.
Hand-quilted by Lou Weibe and Sue Reimer.

1930s Nine-Patch

As the only quilter in my generation, I inherited Great-Grandmother Marsh's quilting box.

It contained Nine-Patch blocks and pastel fabrics typical of the 1930s. I used all the blocks

in this small quilt, setting them on point to make as large a quilt as possible. The green

fabric also came out of the box, and I added muslin for the alternate blocks.

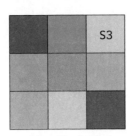

Nine-Patch Block

Materials

	Fabric A (assorted prints and solids)	1⅜ yards total
	Fabric B (green)	¾ yard
	Fabric C (muslin)	1¼ yards
	Binding (dark green)	½ yard
	Backing fabric	1⅞ yards
	Precut batting	45" x 60"

* This quilt is a crib size or wall hanging. Requirements for other sizes are listed below.

Cutting

Instructions are for rotary cutting. To check cutting accuracy, compare rotary-cut pieces to patterns S3, S14, T15, and T16 (see pattern index, page 146). For traditional piecing, use these patterns to make templates.

If you don't have authentic 1930s fabrics, you can duplicate the look with reproduction fabrics. Or sort through your scraps for pastels, looking for solids or small- and medium-scale prints in light, clear colors. The green fabric in this quilt is typical of Depression-era quilts, and similar fabrics are widely available today.

From Fabric A (assorted prints and solids), cut:
• 432 (2") squares (S3), 8 for each block.

From Fabric B (green), cut:
• 54 (2") squares (S3), 1 for each block.
• 7 (7⅝") squares. Cut each square in quarters diagonally to get 26 quarter-square triangles (T15) for side set triangles (and 2 extra).
• 2 (4") squares. Cut each square in half diagonally to get 4 corner set triangles (T16).

From Fabric C (muslin), cut:
• 40 (5") squares (S14) for alternate set squares.

Making Blocks

1. For each block, select 8 squares of Fabric A and 1 square of Fabric B.
2. Join squares in 3 rows of 3 squares each, placing B square at center *(Block Assembly Diagram)*. In top and bottom rows, press seam allowances toward outside edges. In center row, press seam allowances toward green square.
3. Join rows to complete 1 Nine-Patch block. Repeat to make a total of 54 blocks. *(continued)*

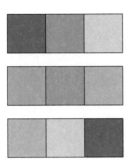

Block Assembly Diagram

Size Variations

	Twin	Full/Queen	King
Finished Size	64" x 83"	83" x 89"	95½" x 95½"
Number of Blocks	130	182	225
Blocks Set	10 x 13	13 x 14	15 x 15
Number of Set Squares	108	156	196
Number of Side Set Triangles	42	50	56

Materials for Size Variations

		Twin	Full/Queen	King
	Fabric A	3 yards	3¾ yards	5⅛ yards
	Fabric B	1 yard	1¼ yards	1½ yards
	Fabric C	2⅛ yards	3 yards	3¾ yards
	Binding	⅝ yard	¾ yard	¾ yard
	Backing	4¼ yards	5¼ yards	9 yards

Quilt Assembly

To assemble this quilt, set blocks on the diagonal, alternating with square set pieces. Set triangles fill in around the edge of the quilt.

1. Lay out Nine-Patch blocks in diagonal rows, alternating blocks with set squares *(Quilt Assembly Diagram)*. Position a set triangle at end of each row as shown. Arrange blocks for a pleasing balance of color and contrast.

2. Join blocks and set pieces in diagonal rows as shown. Press seam allowances toward set pieces.

3. Join rows.

Finishing

1. Mark quilting design on quilt top as desired. On quilt shown, straight-line quilting is accented by small motifs in some alternate squares. Two other quilting suggestions are shown here *(Alternate Quilting Diagrams)*.

2. Layer backing, batting, and quilt top. Baste. Quilt as marked or as desired.

3. Cut 5½ yards of 1½"-wide bias binding. See page 26 for instructions on making and applying binding.

Quilt Assembly Diagram

Alternate Quilting Diagrams

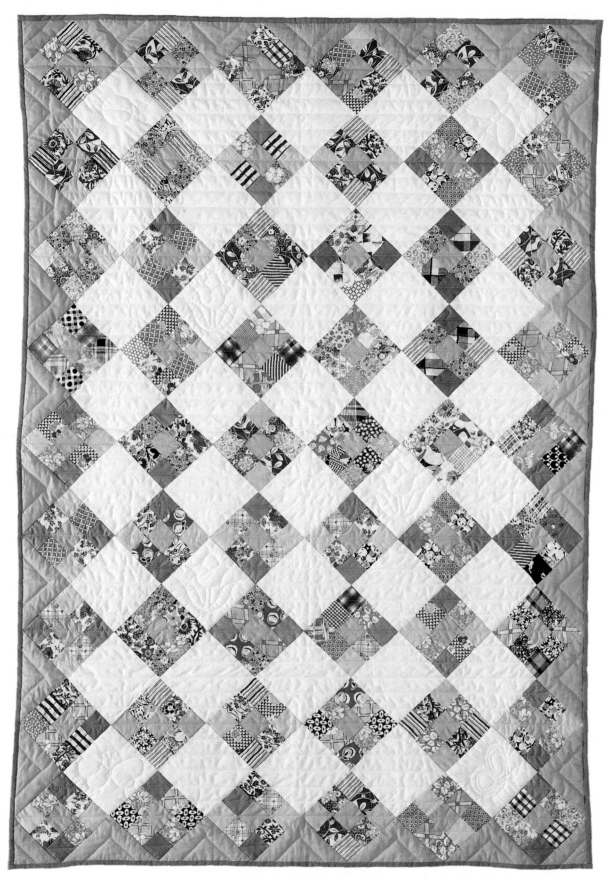

1930s Nine-Patch by Marsha McCloskey, Seattle, Washington, 1986.
Hand-quilted by Freda Smith.

Judy's Nine-Patch

Judy Pollard makes quilts for all the important occasions in the lives of her friends.

She made this happy Nine-Patch quilt as a wedding gift. She chose an easy-to-make design

so she could finish the quilt in time for the couple to use in their first year of marriage.

Judy chose blue and red fabrics for the blocks, including lots of plaids for a country look.

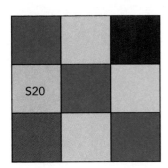

Nine-Patch Block

Materials

	Fabric A (assorted dark prints)	1 yard total
	Fabric B (assorted light prints)	1 yard total
	Fabric C (light print or muslin)	2 yards
	Fabric D (dark blue print)	⅝ yard
	Fabric E (blue plaid)	2⅛ yards
	Binding	⅝ yard
	Backing fabric	3⅝ yards
	Precut batting	72" x 90"

* This quilt fits a twin bed. Requirements for other sizes are listed on page 48.

Cutting

Instructions are for rotary cutting. To check cutting accuracy, compare rotary-cut pieces to patterns S15 and S20 (see pattern index, page 146). For traditional piecing, use these patterns to make templates.

You can strip-piece this block, but Judy cut individual squares so she could arrange them for color before making each block.

From Fabric A (dark prints), cut:
• 195 (2½") squares (S20), 5 for each block.

From Fabric B (light prints), cut:
• 156 (2½") squares (S20), 4 for each block.

From Fabric C (light print), cut:
• 4 (1½" x 70") lengthwise strips for inner border.
• 38 (6½") squares for alternate set squares (S15).

From Fabric D (dark blue), cut:
• 8 (2"-wide) crosswise strips for middle border.

From Fabric E (blue plaid), cut:
• 4 (6½" x 76") lengthwise strips for outer border.

Making Blocks

1. For each Nine-Patch block, select 5 squares of Fabric A and 4 squares of Fabric B.

2. Join squares in 3 rows of 3 squares each *(Block Assembly Diagram)*, placing light and dark squares as shown. In each row, press seam allowances toward darker fabrics.

3. Join rows to complete 1 Nine-Patch block. Repeat to make a total of 39 blocks.

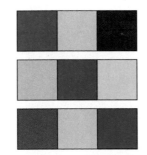

Block Assembly Diagram

Quilt Assembly

1. Lay out blocks in horizontal rows, alternating blocks with set squares *(Row Assembly Diagram)*. Arrange blocks for a pleasing balance of color and contrast.

2. To make Row 1, join 4 Nine-Patch blocks and 3 set squares in a row as shown. Make 6 of Row 1. Press seam allowances toward set squares.

3. To make Row 2, join 3 Nine-Patch blocks and 4 set squares in a row as shown. Make 5 of Row 2. Press seam allowances toward set squares.

4. Starting with Row 1, join rows, alternating rows 1 and 2.

Adding Borders

1. Referring to instructions on page 20, measure quilt from top to bottom; then trim 2 Fabric C border strips to match length. Join borders to sides of quilt. Press seam allowances toward borders. *(continued)*

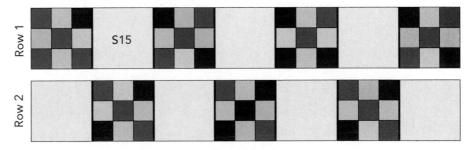

Row Assembly Diagram

2. Measure quilt from side to side; then trim remaining Fabric C borders to match quilt width. Join borders to top and bottom edges. Press seam allowances toward borders.

3. For middle border, join pairs of Fabric D strips end-to-end to make 4 border strips. Join borders to quilt in same manner as for first border.

4. Join Fabric E border strips to quilt.

Finishing

1. Mark quilting design on quilt top as desired. On quilt shown, diagonal lines of machine quilting make an X through each Nine-Patch and a heart motif is quilted in alternate squares.

2. Divide backing fabric into 2 equal lengths. Join lengths to make backing.

3. Layer backing, batting, and quilt top. (Backing seam will run parallel to top and bottom edges of quilt top.) Baste. Quilt as marked or as desired.

4. Cut 8 yards of 1½"-wide bias binding. See page 26 for instructions on making and applying binding.

Size Variations

	Crib	Full/Queen	King
Finished Size	47" x 47"	83" x 95"	95" x 95"
Number of Nine-Patch Blocks	13	72	85
Number of Set Squares	12	71	84
Blocks Set	5 x 5	11 x 13	13 x 13

Materials for Size Variations

		Crib	Full/Queen	King
	Fabric A	⅜ yard	1⅝ yards	2 yards
	Fabric B	⅜ yard	1½ yards	1¾ yards
	Fabric C	¾ yard*	2¾ yards	3⅛ yards
	Fabric D*	¼ yard	⅝ yard	⅝ yard
	Fabric E	1½ yards	2½ yards	2⅞ yards
	Binding fabric	½ yard	¾ yard	¾ yard
	Backing fabric	2¾ yards	6 yards	8¾ yards

* Cut strips crosswise.

Judy's Nine-Patch by Judy Pollard, Seattle, Washington, 1995.
Machine-quilted by Lynn Baxter.

Grandmother's Dream

This quilt is a variation of an old favorite called Trip Around the World. Reynola Pakusich

used solid fabrics for a traditional Amish look. She pieced the center of the quilt

in sections. Once you choose fabrics, you'll find the cutting and piecing go quickly.

Cutting

Instructions are for rotary cutting. To check cutting accuracy, compare rotary-cut pieces to patterns S3, T3, and T22 (see pattern index, page 146). For traditional piecing, use these patterns to make templates.

From Fabric A (black), cut:
• 49 (2") squares (S3).
• 21 (3⅜") squares. Cut each square in quarters diagonally to get 84 quarter-square triangles (T3) for outside edges of Unit 1.
• 2 (1¹⁵⁄₁₆") squares. Cut each square in half diagonally to get 4 half-square triangles (T22) for ends of Unit 2.

From Fabric B (dark green), cut:
• 2 (10½" x 68") and 2 (10½" x 88") lengthwise strips for outer borders.
• 48 (2") squares (S3).

From Fabric C (gray-green), cut:
• 8 (2") squares (S3).

From Fabric D (dark red), cut:
• 260 (2") squares (S3).
• 2 (33⅞") squares. Cut each square in half diagonally to get 4 large half-square triangles.

From Fabric E (light pink), cut:
• 148 (2") squares (S3).

From Fabric F (rose), cut:
• 152 (2") squares (S3).

From Fabric G (dark rose), cut:
• 24 (2") squares (S3).

From Fabric H (red), cut:
• 160 (2") squares (S3).

From Fabric I (mint green), cut:
• 36 (2") squares (S3).

From Fabric J (dark blue-green), cut:
• 40 (2") squares (S3).

Approximate finished size: 86" x 86"*

Materials

■	Fabric A (black)	½ yard
■	Fabric B (dark green)	2⅞ yards
■	Fabric C (gray-green)	⅛ yard
■	Fabric D (dark red)	2½ yards
■	Fabric E (light pink)	½ yard
■	Fabric F (rose)	½ yard
■	Fabric G (dark rose)	⅛ yard
■	Fabric H (red)	½ yard
■	Fabric I (mint green)	¼ yard
■	Fabric J (dark blue-green)	⅛ yard
	Binding (red)	¾ yard
	Backing fabric	5¼ yards
	Precut batting	90" x 108"

* This quilt fits a full or queen-size bed. To adapt this design for other sizes, adjust width of border as desired.

Making Unit 1

Instructions are for chain-piecing. The secret to making this quilt is to keep the squares in the correct color sequence. To keep them in order, stack squares on a tray with appropriate labels so you can pick up the correct squares easily as you sew.

There are 4 of Unit 1, which is a large pieced triangle consisting of 21 rows of squares and a T3 at the end of each row. Each row has 1 less square than the row before.

Unit 1 Row Assembly Diagram shows how you can chain-piece rows 1–21 in vertical bands of color that will be offset when you join rows. The first color band is 1 square of Fabric C (gray-green), which appears at the upper left corner of Unit 1. The second vertical color band is 2 squares of Fabric D (dark red), followed by 3 squares of Fabric E (pink), and so on. As you chain-piece, add squares of the same color band to each row. The last square in the color band becomes the start of a new row.

Do not cut threads (chains) between rows. Leaving rows attached keeps them in order as the piecing continues. Do not press until unit is complete.

1. To start Row 1, sew 1 C (gray-green) square to 1 D (dark red) square. Another D square begins Row 2.

2. The next color band is 3 E (pink) squares. Chain-piece 1 E square to the right of both D squares. The third E square begins Row 3.

3. The fourth color band is 4 F (rose) squares. Chain-piece 1 F square to end of each preceding row. The fourth F square begins Row 4.

4. Referring to diagram, add each color band as shown. Each color band adds 1 square to existing rows and begins a new row. Continue in this manner until you have 20 rows as shown.

5. Add a T3 to end of each row. Row 21 is a T3 without any squares.

6. Clip rows 1 and 2 from chain. Finger-press Row 1 seam allowances away from triangle end of row; then press Row 2 seam allowances toward triangle.

7. With right sides facing, match squares on both rows at left side (they've been offset by 1 square until now). Pin if necessary. Join rows.

8. Add each row, matching squares at left side of unit. Always press seam allowances in opposite direction from previous row, so seam allowances alternate row by row. Join 21 rows to complete Unit 1 *(Unit 1 Diagram)*.

9. Repeat to make a total of 4 units. It is important that seam allowances are pressed in the same manner on all 4 units, starting with seam allowances pressed away from triangle on Row 1. When units are joined, seam allowances will be properly opposed all around.

Making Unit 2

There are 4 of Unit 2, which is a row of 21 squares and 1 triangle *(Unit 2 Assembly Diagram)*.

1. Begin by chain-piecing 4 C (gray-green) squares to 4 B (dark green) squares. Do not cut chains.

2. Add 1 D (dark red) square to each C square.

3. Continue adding squares, moving to the right across each row and following color order as shown until each row is 21 squares long.

4. Add 1 T22 triangle to end of each row.

5. Cut chains to separate 4 rows. Press seam allowances toward triangle end of each row. *(continued)*

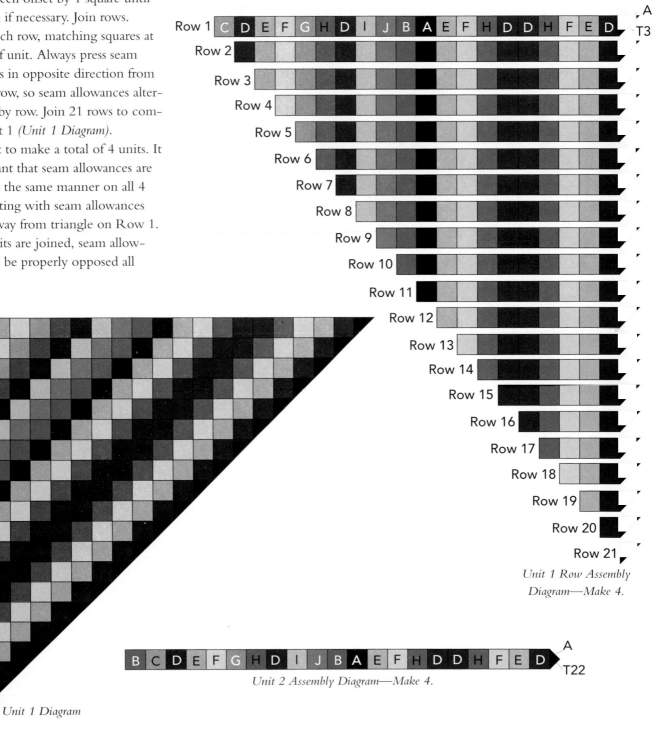

Unit 1 Row Assembly Diagram—Make 4.

Unit 1 Diagram

Unit 2 Assembly Diagram—Make 4.

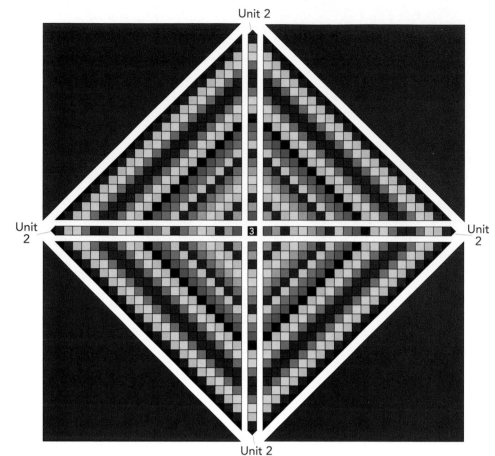

Quilt Assembly Diagram

Quilt Assembly

1. Lay out 4 of Unit 1 *(Quilt Assembly Diagram)*, turning triangles toward outside edge of medallion as shown. Place Unit 2s as shown, with Unit 3 (a single black square) in center.

2. Join top pair of Unit 1s to sides of Unit 2. Join bottom pair of Units 1s to sides of Unit 2. Press seam allowances away from Unit 2s.

3. Join remaining pair of Unit 2s to Unit 3 square. Press seam allowances toward Unit 3.

4. Join 3 sections to complete pieced medallion.

5. Add a Fabric D triangle to opposite sides of medallion. Press seam allowances toward triangles. Add triangles to remaining sides of medallion.

Adding Borders

1. Referring to instructions on page 20, measure quilt from top to bottom; then trim 68"-long borders to match length. Join borders to quilt sides.

2. Measure quilt from side to side; then trim remaining borders to match quilt width. Join borders to top and bottom edges. Press seam allowances toward borders.

Finishing

1. Mark quilting designs on quilt top as desired. The large plain triangles and the borders are ideal places to showcase fancy quilting. Check your favorite quilt shop or mail-order catalog for feather stencils that will fit these areas. The pieced center of the quilt is quilted in diagonal lines that make an X through alternate squares.

2. Divide backing fabric into 2 (2⅝-yard) lengths. Join lengths to make backing. Layer backing, batting, and quilt top. Baste. Quilt as marked or as desired.

3. Cut 10 yards of 1½"-wide bias binding. See page 26 for instructions on making and applying binding.

Using a Seam Ripper

Keep a seam ripper next to your sewing machine so you can undo mistakes. Don't try to rip a seam, though. Slip the seam ripper blade under a stitch to snap it. Break every third stitch along the seam, and then you can separate the two fabrics without undue stress on the fabric or the quilter.

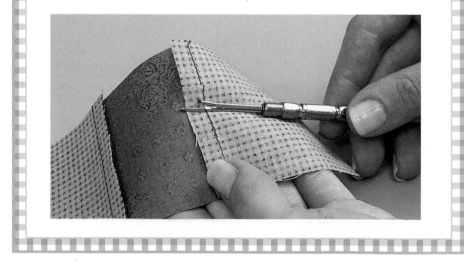

Grandmother's Dream by Reynola Pakusich, Bellingham, Washington, 1988.
Hand-quilted by Hazel Montague.

Burgoyne Surrounded

This quilt is a good exercise in strip piecing. You'll often find antique Burgoyne Surrounded

quilts worked in indigo or red and white, similar in style to 19th-century woven coverlets.

Terri Shinn's quilt is scrappy, with assorted navy fabrics in a traditional light and dark arrangement.

The variety gives the quilt a more complex look than a simple two-fabric treatment.

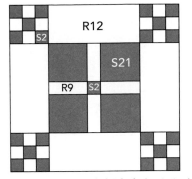

Burgoyne Surrounded Block (variation)

Approximate finished size: 89" x 109" • Blocks: 12 (16¼") blocks

Materials

	Fabric A (assorted navy prints)	3¼ yards total
	Fabric B (light print or muslin)	4¼ yards
	Fabric C (dark navy for borders, binding)	4 yards total
	Backing fabric	8¼ yards
	Precut batting	120" x 120"

* This quilt fits a full or queen-size bed. Requirements for other sizes are listed on page 58.

Cutting

Instructions are for rotary cutting. To check cutting accuracy, compare rotary-cut pieces to patterns S2, S21, R9, and R12 (see pattern index, page 146). For traditional piecing, use these patterns to make templates.

Note: Cut all strips crosswise except as noted.

From Fabric A (navy prints), cut:
• 45 (1¾"-wide) strips for strip sets 1, 2, and 4.
• 6 (4¼"-wide) strips for Strip Set 3.

From Fabric B (light print), cut:
• 37 (1¾"-wide) strips for strip sets 1, 2, and 3.
• 18 (4¼"-wide) strips. From 17 of these, cut 48 (4¼" x 9¼") rectangles (R12) and 62 (4¼") squares (S21). Cut remaining strip in half (4¼" x 22") for Strip Set 4.

Fabric C (dark navy), cut:
• 10 (4¼" x 108") lengthwise strips. Set aside 8 strips for borders. (If desired, piece borders from different fabrics to achieve length needed.) From remaining 2 strips, cut 14 (4¼" x 9¼") rectangles (R12) and 18 (4¼") squares (S21).
• 1 (27") square for binding.

Making Unit X (Nine-Patch)

1. To make Strip Set 1, join 2 (1¾"-wide) Fabric A strips to both sides of 1 Fabric B strip (*Strip Set 1 Diagram*). Press seam allowances toward Fabric A strips. Make 18 of Strip Set 1.
2. Make Strip Set 2 in same manner, joining 2 strips of Fabric B to both sides of 1 Fabric A strip (*Strip Set 2 Diagram*). Press seam allowances toward Fabric A. Repeat to make 8 of Strip Set 2.
3. From each Strip Set 1, cut 3 or 4 (4¼"-wide) segments to get a total of 62 segments. Set these aside for lattice units. From remaining Strip Set 1s, cut 248 (1¾"-wide) segments. Set 48 of these aside for pieced border.
4. From Strip Set 2s, cut 179 (1¾"-wide) segments. Set aside 31 segments for lattice units and 48 segments for pieced border.
5. You should have left 200 segments of Strip Set 1 and 100 segments of Strip Set 2 for Unit X. Unit X is a Nine-Patch. For each unit, join 2 Strip Set 1 segments and 1 Strip Set 2 segment (*Unit X Diagram*). Make 100 of Unit X.

Making Unit Y

1. To make Strip Set 3, join 2 (4¼"-wide) Fabric A strips to both sides of 1 (1¾"-wide) Fabric B strip (*Strip Set 3 Diagram*). Press seam allowances toward Fabric A. Repeat to make 3 of Strip Set 3. *(continued)*

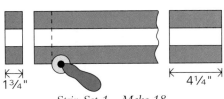

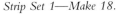

Strip Set 1—Make 18.

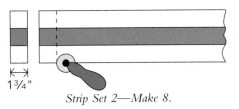

Strip Set 2—Make 8.

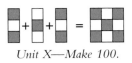

Unit X—Make 100.

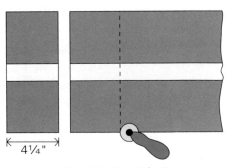

Strip Set 3—Make 3.

2. To make Strip Set 4, join 2 (4¼" x 22") strips of Fabric B to both sides of 1 Fabric A strip *(Strip Set 4 Diagram)*. Press seam allowances toward Fabric A.

3. From each Strip Set 3, cut 8 (4¼"-wide) segments to get a total of 24 segments.

4. From Strip Set 4, cut 12 (1¾"-wide) segments.

5. For each unit, join 2 Strip Set 3 segments and 1 Strip Set 4 segment *(Unit Y Diagram)*. Make 12 of Unit Y.

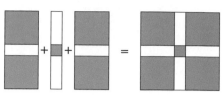

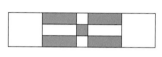

1¾"

Strip Set 4—Make 1.

Unit Y—Make 12.

Making Blocks

1. For each block, select 4 of Unit X, 1 of Unit Y, and 4 (4¼" x 9¼") Fabric B strips.

2. Join 2 Fabric B strips to opposite sides of Unit Y *(Block Assembly Diagram)*. Press seam allowances toward strips.

3. Join 2 of Unit X to ends of each remaining strip as shown. Press seam allowances toward strip.

4. Join sections to complete 1 block. Repeat to make a total of 12 blocks.

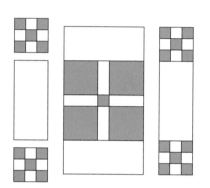

Block Assembly Diagram

Lattice Unit—Make 31.

Making Lattice Units

1. Join 2 (4¼"-wide) segments from Strip Set 1 to both sides of 1 Strip Set 2 segment *(Lattice Unit Diagram)*. Press seam allowances toward Strip Set 1 segments.

2. Join Fabric B squares to ends as shown to complete Lattice Unit. Press seam allowance toward Fabric B squares. Repeat to make a total of 31 Lattice Units.

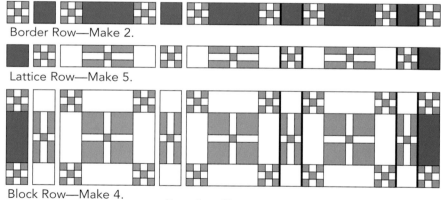

Border Row—Make 2.

Lattice Row—Make 5.

Block Row—Make 4.

Row Assembly Diagram

Quilt Assembly

1. For top Border Row (see photo), select 8 of Unit X (Nine-Patch), 4 Fabric C squares, and 3 Fabric C rectangles. Join units in a row *(Row Assembly Diagram)*. Repeat for bottom Border Row.

2. For each Lattice Row, select 3 Lattice Units, 4 of Unit X, and 2 Fabric C squares. Join units in a row as shown. Repeat to make 5 Lattice Rows.

3. Each Block Row has 2 Border Units. For each Border Unit, select 2 of Unit X and 1 Fabric C rectangle. Sew 1 Unit X to ends of each rectangle and press seam allowances toward rectangle. Repeat to make 10 Border Units.

4. For each Block Row, select 3 blocks, 4 Lattice Units, and 2 Border Units. Join units in a row as shown. Repeat to make 4 Block Rows.

5. Starting with 3 rows shown, join rows (see photo). Lattice Rows and Block Rows alternate down length of quilt, ending with second Border Row. *(continued)*

Burgoyne Surrounded by Terri Shinn for her daughter Heather's 16th birthday, Snohomish, Washington, 1995. Design by Marsha McCloskey.

Adding Borders

1. Referring to instructions on page 20, measure quilt from top to bottom; then trim 2 Fabric C border strips to match length. Join borders to quilt sides. Press seam allowances toward borders.

2. Measure quilt from side to side; then trim 2 Fabric C border strips to match quilt width. Join borders to top and bottom edges. Press seam allowances toward borders.

3. Use remaining segments of strip sets 1 and 2 for pieced borders. For 1 side border, start with a Strip Set 2 segment and alternate 1s and 2s to join 26 segments. Cut 1 (1¾") square of Fabric B and join it to bottom of border so that border has Fabric B squares at both ends. Repeat to make second side border. Join borders to quilt sides, easing to fit as necessary.

4. Assemble top pieced border in same manner, starting with a Strip Set 1 segment and alternating 1s and 2s to join 22 segments. Remove B square from last Strip Set 2 segment so that border has Fabric A squares at both ends. Repeat to make bottom border. Join borders to top and bottom edges. Press seam allowances toward inner border.

5. Repeat steps 1 and 2 to join outer borders of Fabric C.

Finishing

1. Mark quilting design on quilt top as desired. Quilt shown has Baptist Fan quilting (see page 23). Two other quilting suggestions are shown here *(Alternate Quilting Diagrams)*.

2. Divide backing into 3 (2¾-yard) lengths. Join lengths to make 1 (99" x 126") backing. Layer backing, batting, and quilt top. (Backing seams will parallel top and bottom edges of quilt.) Baste. Quilt as marked or as desired.

3. Cut 11¼ yards of 1½"-wide bias binding. See page 26 for instructions on making and applying binding.

Size Variations

	Twin	King
Finished Size	69" x 89"	109" x 109"
Number of Blocks	6	16
Blocks Set	2 x 3	4 x 4
Number of Unit X	60	121
Number of Unit Y	6	16
Number of Lattice Units	17	40
Number of Strip Set 1	10	21
Number of Strip Set 2	5	9
Number of Strip Set 3	2	4
Number of Strip Set 4	1	1

Materials for Size Variations

		Twin	King
	Fabric A	2 yards	5⅜ yards
	Fabric B	2½ yards	5¼ yards
	Fabric C	2¾ yards	4¼ yards
	Backing fabric	5½ yards	10 yards
	Binding	⅝ yard	⅞ yard

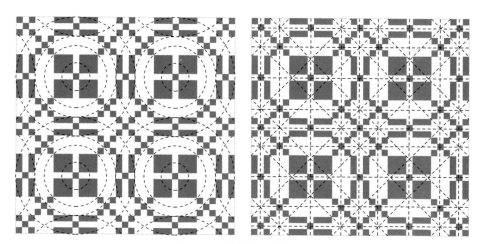

Alternate Quilting Diagrams

Care and Cleaning

A quilt's greatest enemies are light and dirt. To keep your quilt in pristine condition would mean never using it and storing it in ideal archival conditions—to which I say, "What's the point?" We make quilts to use and enjoy.

Safekeeping

If you display a quilt, it is bound to fade over time. But you can minimize the fading by keeping the quilt out of strong sunlight and storing it properly when not in use.

Rotate the quilt in use with others every few months to reduce exposure. Store an unused quilt—with as few folds as possible—in a cotton pillowcase. Don't use plastic bags, which trap moisture. To prevent permanent creases, air and refold stored quilts occasionally. Wads of acid-free paper inside the folds also discourage creases.

Washing

Wash quilts infrequently. A good airing is usually all that's needed to freshen a quilt. You can vacuum wall quilts. Dry cleaning is bad for most quilts because it can leave harmful chemicals in the fibers.

When you must wash a quilt, use a mild soap such as Ensure or Orvis Paste (a shampoo originally designed for livestock). These soaps (as well as acid-free paper and boxes) are available at quilt shops and from mail-order sources.

A Good Soak. Wash large quilts by hand in the bathtub. Fill the tub with luke-warm water, adding the amount of soap specified on the label. Immerse the quilt and gently agitate it with your hands to disperse the soap. Let the quilt soak for 15–20 minutes; then drain the tub.

Squeeze as much water out of the quilt as possible, but don't wring or twist the quilt because this puts undue stress on stitches and fabric. Fill the tub with clear water to rinse. Let the quilt soak a few minutes; then drain the tub again and squeeze out excess water. Rinse repeatedly until the water runs clear.

Drying. Squeeze out the rinse water. Carefully lift the quilt out of the tub, supporting all its weight. Place the quilt flat between two mattress pads (or a lot of towels), and roll it up to remove as much moisture as possible.

Lay the damp quilt flat to dry. If you want to dry it outside, pick a shady spot on a sunny day, and place the quilt between bedsheets to protect it from the ground and overflying birds. When the quilt is almost dry, and if it isn't too large, you can put it in the dryer on cool or air settings to smooth out wrinkles and fluff it up a bit.

Sunshine-in-the-Window Log Cabin

An easy block for a beginner, Log Cabin was a favorite of mine early in my quilting career.

I was inspired to return to this all-time classic by a 1930s quilt I saw in Illinois. Since most

Log Cabins have red centers, symbolizing the hearth as the center of the home, yellow

centers really caught my eye. It's the yellow that gives this variation its charming name.

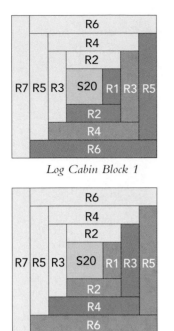

Log Cabin Block 1

Log Cabin Block 2

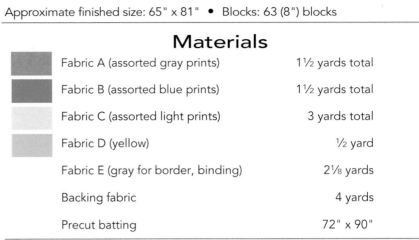

Approximate finished size: 65" x 81" • Blocks: 63 (8") blocks

Materials

	Fabric A (assorted gray prints)	1½ yards total
	Fabric B (assorted blue prints)	1½ yards total
	Fabric C (assorted light prints)	3 yards total
	Fabric D (yellow)	½ yard
	Fabric E (gray for border, binding)	2⅛ yards
	Backing fabric	4 yards
	Precut batting	72" x 90"

* This quilt fits a twin bed. Requirements for other sizes are listed on page 62.

Cutting

Instructions are for rotary cutting. To check cutting accuracy, compare rotary-cut pieces to patterns S20 and R1–R7 (see pattern index, page 146). For traditional piecing, use these patterns to make templates.

Note: Cut all strips lengthwise. Fat quarters are ideal for cutting these strips. When cutting strips into pieces for blocks, don't cut all of the same piece from the same fabric; instead, cut from as many varied fabrics as possible to scatter fabric positions randomly across the quilt.

From Fabric A (gray prints), cut:
• 63 (1½" x 18") strips. From these, cut 32 *each* of R1 (2½" long), R2 (3½" long), R3 (4½" long), R4 (5½" long), R5 (6½" long), and R6 (7½" long).

From Fabric B (blue prints), cut:
• 63 (1½" x 18") strips. From these, cut 32 *each* of R1 (2½" long), R2 (3½" long), R3 (4½" long), R4 (5½" long), R5 (6½" long), and R6 (7½" long).

From Fabric C (light prints), cut:
• 126 (1½" x 18") strips. From these, cut 126 *each* of R2 (3½" long), R3 (4½" long), R4 (5½" long), R5 (6½" long), R6 (7½" long), and R7 (8½" long).

From Fabric D (yellow), cut:
• 63 (2½") squares (S20).

From Fabric E (gray), cut:
• 4 (5" x 75") strips for border.
• 1 (23") square for binding.

Making Blocks

In this quilt, 2 blocks alternate to create ripples of gray and blue in diagonal lines of color. Both blocks are sewn in the same manner, but Block 1 emphasizes blue fabrics while Block 2 has more gray. Light fabrics are random, including blue, gray, yellow, and a little pink for interest.

1. For each Block 1, select 1 each of pieces R2, R3, R4, R5, R6, and R7 from light fabrics and 1 yellow square. From blue fabrics, select 1 each of pieces R1, R2, R5, and R6. From gray fabrics, select 1 each of pieces R3 and R4. Referring to photo and *Block*

Diagrams, note that adjacent strips of the same color are usually of the same fabric. (For example, strips R1 and R2 are of the same blue fabric, while strips R5 and R6 are a matched pair of another blue print.)

2. Join blue R1 to 1 side of square. Press seam allowances toward R1.

3. Join light R2 and blue R2 to top and bottom edges of square *(Diagram A)*. Press seam allowances toward R2s.

4. Join light R3 and gray R3 to sides of unit *(Diagram B)*. Press seam allowances toward R3s.   *(continued)*

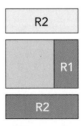

Diagram A

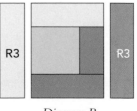

Diagram B

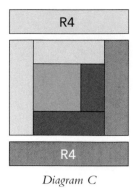

Diagram C

5. Join light R4 and gray R4 to top and bottom edges of unit *(Diagram C)*. Press seam allowances toward R4s. Add R5s and R6s to opposite edges of unit in same manner. Complete block with light R7 strip.

6. Repeat to make a total of 31 of Block 1.

7. Make 32 of Block 2 in same manner, switching positions of gray and blue fabrics as shown in *Block Diagram*.

Quilt Assembly

Log Cabin blocks can be set many ways, and each set has a descriptive name. These instructions are for the Straight Furrows set shown. Before joining blocks, play with light/dark arrangements as desired to see if you find a set that you prefer.

1. To make Row 1, join 4 of Block 2 and 3 of Block 1 *(Row Assembly Diagram)*. Turn all Block 2s upside-down as shown, so you're always sewing light strips to lights and blue strips to grays. Make 5 of Row 1.

2. To make Row 2, join 4 of Block 1 and 3 of Block 2 as shown. Make 4 of Row 2.

3. Starting with a Row 1, join rows, alternating rows 1 and 2.

Adding Borders

1. Referring to instructions on page 20, measure quilt from top to bottom; then trim 2 border strips to match length. Join borders to quilt sides. Press seam allowances toward borders.

2. Measure quilt from side to side;

Size Variations

	Full	Queen	King
Finished Size	81" x 97"	89" x 97"	97" x 105"
Number of Blocks	99	110	132
Blocks Set	9 x 11	10 x 11	11 x 12

Materials for Size Variations

		Full	Queen	King
	Fabric A	2 yards	2¼ yards	2½ yards
	Fabric B	2 yards	2¼ yards	2½ yards
	Fabric C	4 yards	4¼ yards	5 yards
	Fabric D	⅝ yard	⅝ yard	¾ yard
	Fabric E	2⅝ yards	2⅝ yards	2⅞ yards
	Backing fabric	6 yards	8¼ yards	9 yards

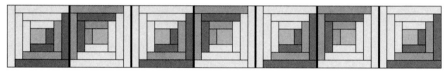

Row 1—Make 5.

Row 2—Make 4.

Row Assembly Diagram

then trim remaining borders to match quilt width. Join borders to top and bottom edges. Press seam allowances toward borders.

Finishing

1. Mark quilting design on quilt top as desired. Quilt shown has Baptist Fan quilting (see page 23). Two other quilting suggestions are shown here *(Alternate Quilting Diagrams)*.

2. Divide backing fabric into 2 (2-yard) lengths. Join lengths to make backing. Layer backing, batting, and quilt top. Backing seam parallels top and bottom edges of quilt. Baste. Quilt as marked or as desired.

3. Cut 6 yards of 1½"-wide bias binding. See page 26 for instructions on making and applying binding.

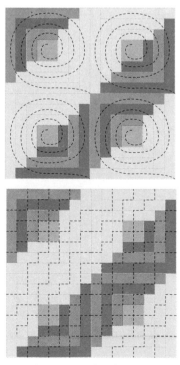

Alternate Quilting Diagrams

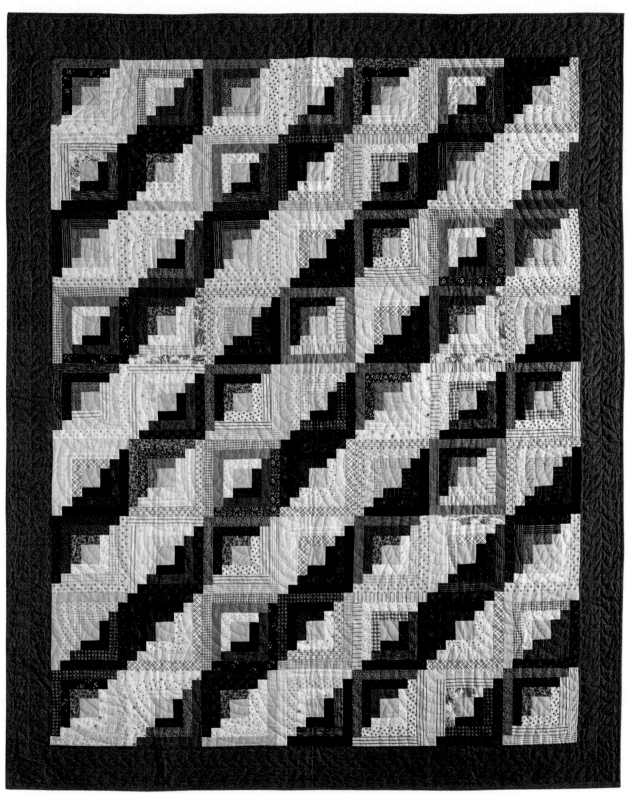

Sunshine-in-the-Window Log Cabin by Marsha McCloskey,
Seattle, Washington, 1994.

Flying Geese & Stars

I cut and pieced this quilt top in just a few days, using four yellows, two reds, and several golds. I chose fabrics from

my collection, but I found I didn't have enough of any one print, so I switched to similar ones as I went along.

Running out of fabric can be a good thing if it makes your choices more varied and interesting.

In this traditional Flying Geese pattern, red stars appear where the units come together.

Approximate finished size: 65½" x 83½"* • Blocks: 48 (4¼" x 8½") blocks

Flying Geese Block

Materials

■	Fabric A (assorted red prints)	2¼ yards total
■	Fabric B (assorted light yellow prints)	1¼ yards total
■	Fabric C (green print)	1½ yards
■	Fabric D (assorted gold prints)	2⅛ yards total
	Binding fabric	¾ yard
	Backing fabric	4 yards
	Precut batting	72" x 90"

* This quilt fits a twin bed. Requirements for other sizes are on page 66.

Cutting

Instructions are for rotary cutting. To check cutting accuracy, compare rotary-cut pieces to patterns S5, T5, T9, and T19 (see pattern index, page 146). For traditional piecing, use these patterns to make templates.

From Fabric A (red prints), cut:
• 4 (6" x 81") lengthwise strips for outer border.
• 12 (4¾") squares (S5) for star centers.
• 48 (3") squares. Cut each square in half diagonally to get 96 half-square triangles (T9) for star points. For easy matching, trim points at 2⅝" (see page 13).

From Fabric B (yellow prints), cut:
• 48 (5½") squares. Cut each square in quarters diagonally to get 192 quarter-square triangles (T19), 4 for each block.

From Fabric C (green print), cut:
• 3 (7¼") squares. Cut each square in quarters diagonally to get 10 quarter-square triangles (T5) for small side set triangles (and 2 extra).
• 6 (4¾") squares (S5) for small set squares.
• 2 (3⅞") squares. Cut each square in half diagonally to get 4 half-square triangles (T19) for corner set pieces.
• 144 (3") squares. Cut each square in half diagonally to get 288 half-square triangles (T9) for Flying Geese units. Trim points at 2⅝".

From Fabric D (gold prints), cut:
• 4 (13¼") squares. Cut each square in quarters diagonally to get 14 quarter-square triangles for large side set triangles (and 2 extra).
• 17 (9") squares for large set squares.

Making Blocks

You might not find this "block" in an encyclopedia of quilt designs, but I'm calling each four-geese section a block for ease of assembling this quilt.

1. For each block, select 2 Fabric A T9 triangles, 6 Fabric C T9 triangles, and 4 Fabric B T19 triangles.

2. Flying Geese units are easy to make—just sew a T9 triangle to both short legs of each T19 triangle (*Block Assembly Diagram*). Press seam allowances toward smaller triangles. Make 4 geese, 3 with Fabric C corners and 1 with Fabric A corners as shown.

3. Join geese in a row as shown to complete block.

4. Repeat to make a total of 48 blocks. *(continued)*

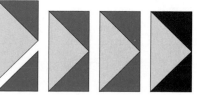

Block Assembly Diagram

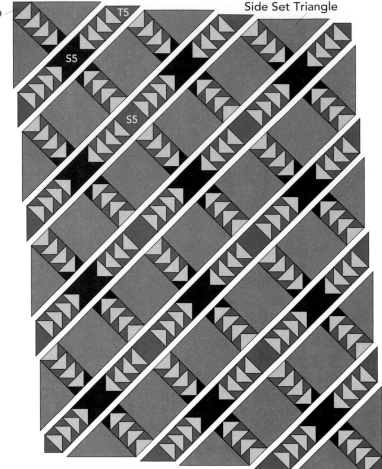

Quilt Assembly Diagram

Quilt Assembly

To assemble this quilt, blocks are set on the diagonal, alternating with square set pieces. Set triangles fill in around the edge of the quilt.

1. Lay out blocks in diagonal rows, alternating blocks with set squares *(Quilt Assembly Diagram)*. Note placement of Fabric A and Fabric C S5 set squares. Position a set triangle at ends of each row as shown. Arrange blocks, set squares, and set triangles to achieve a balance of color and contrast.

2. When satisfied with arrangement, join blocks and set pieces in each diagonal row. Press seam allowances toward set pieces.

3. Join rows as shown.

Adding Border

1. Referring to instructions on page 20, measure quilt from top to bottom; then trim 2 border strips to match length. Join borders to quilt sides. Press seam allowances toward borders.

2. Measure quilt from side to side; then trim remaining borders to match quilt width. Join borders to top and bottom edges. Press seam allowances toward borders.

Size Variations

	Full/Queen	King
Finished Size	83½" x 101½"	101½" x 101½"
Number of Blocks	80	100
Number of		
Large Set Squares	31	40
Large Set Triangles	18	20
T5 Triangles, Fabric C	14	16
S5 Squares, Fabric A	20	25
S5 Squares, Fabric C	12	16

Materials for Size Variations

		Full/Queen	King
	Fabric A	2¾ yards	3 yards
	Fabric B	2 yards	2½ yards
	Fabric C	2⅛ yards	2½ yards
	Fabric D	3 yards	3½ yards
	Binding fabric	¾ yard	¾ yard
	Backing fabric	6 yards	9 yards

Alternate Quilting Diagrams

Flying Geese & Stars by Marsha McCloskey, Seattle, Washington, 1995.
Machine-quilted by Barbara Ford.

Finishing

1. Mark quilting design on quilt top as desired. Quilt shown is quilted in-the–ditch with a scroll motif quilted in set squares and triangles. The border is quilted in a scroll design. Two other quilting suggestions are shown here *(Alternate Quilting Diagrams)*.

2. Divide backing into 2 (2-yard) lengths. Join lengths to assemble backing. Layer backing, batting, and quilt top. (Backing seam will be parallel to top and bottom edges of quilt.) Baste. Quilt as marked or as desired.

3. Cut 10 yards of 1½"-wide bias binding. See page 26 for instructions on making and applying binding.

Little Cedar Tree

I use this pattern as a warm-up project to teach bias-strip piecing. For this little quilt, I chose a variety of vibrant prints that have an old-fashioned look and paired them with lighter prints. Touches of red and yellow give the quilt a festive air. This quilt uses up lots of scraps—you'll need 8" squares of light and dark fabrics.

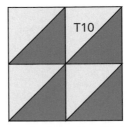

Little Cedar Tree Block

Approximate finished size: 45" x 55" • Blocks: 63 (5") blocks

Materials

Fabric A (assorted dark prints)	1¾ yards total
Fabric B (assorted light prints)	1¾ yards total
Fabric C (navy stripe for border)	1½ yards
Backing fabric	3 yards
Binding fabric	⅝ yard
Precut batting	72" x 90"

* This quilt is a crib size or wall hanging. Requirements for other sizes are listed on page 70.

Cutting

Instructions are for rotary cutting. To check cutting accuracy, compare rotary-cut triangle-squares to Pattern S12 (see pattern index, page 146). For traditional piecing, use Pattern T10 to make templates.

From Fabric A (dark prints), cut:
• 32 (8") squares for bias-strip piecing.

From Fabric B (light prints), cut:
• 32 (8") squares for bias-strip piecing.

From Fabric C (navy stripe), cut:
• 4 (5½" x 54") lengthwise strips for border.

Making Blocks

See page 16 for detailed instructions on bias-strip piecing two-triangle squares.

1. Select 1 Fabric A square and 1 Fabric B square. With right sides facing, match squares.

2. Cutting through both layers, cut squares diagonally from corner to corner to establish true bias (45° angle).

3. Measuring from cut edges, cut 2 sets of 3"-wide strips and 2 sets of left-over corner triangles *(Diagram A)*.

4. Join each pair of bias strips; then join pairs to complete a bias-strip setup as shown *(Diagram B)*. Press seam allowances toward dark fabric.

5. Using a square ruler with bias marking, rotary-cut 7 (3") squares (S12) from this setup, 2 from corners and 5 from strips *(Diagram B)*.

6. To get an eighth triangle-square from this setup, join remaining edge pieces *(Diagram C)* and cut 1 more square. *(continued)*

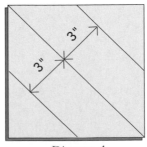

Diagram A

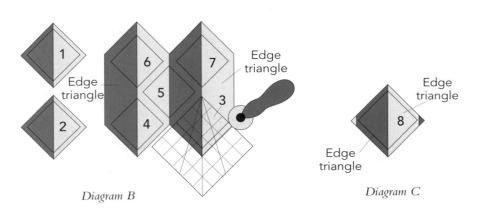

Diagram B

Diagram C

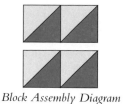

Block Assembly Diagram

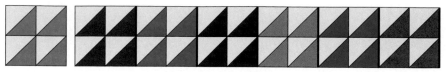

Row Assembly Diagram

7. Repeat with remaining sets of A and B squares to make a total of 252 two-triangle squares. (Each setup makes enough triangle-squares for 2 blocks).

8. For each block, select 4 matching two-triangle squares. Join squares in pairs *(Block Assembly Diagram);* then join pairs to complete block. Repeat to make a total of 63 blocks.

Quilt Assembly

1. Lay out blocks in 9 horizontal rows, with 7 blocks in each row *(Row Assembly Diagram).* Arrange blocks to achieve a pleasing balance of color and contrast.

2. When satisfied with block placement, join blocks in each row. Referring to photo, join rows.

Adding Borders

1. Referring to instructions on page 20, measure quilt from top to bottom. Trim 2 border strips to this length *plus* 5¼" for side borders. Then measure quilt from side to side and trim remaining border strips to this measurement *plus* 5¼" for top and bottom borders.

2. With right sides facing, match end of 1 side border strip to bottom left corner of quilt. Stitch border to quilt edge, stopping about 2" from top corner of quilt. Leave border end unstitched for now.

3. With right sides facing, match end of bottom border strip to bottom edge of quilt and stitch.

4. Match remaining side border to right edge of quilt and stitch. Sew top border in same manner.

5. Complete side border seam at top left corner. Press seam allowances toward borders.

Finishing

1. Mark quilting design on quilt top as desired. On quilt shown, triangles are quilted in-the-ditch and a wave motif is quilted in the outer border. Two other quilting suggestions are shown here *(Alternate Quilting Diagrams).*

2. Divide backing into 2 equal lengths. Join both panels to assemble backing. Layer backing, batting, and quilt top. (Backing seam will parallel top and bottom edges of quilt). Baste. Quilt as marked or as desired.

3. Cut 6 yards of 1½"-wide bias binding. See page 26 for instructions on making and applying binding.

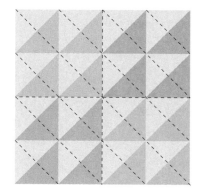 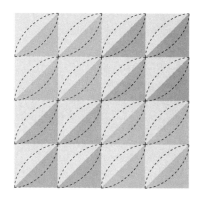

Alternate Quilting Diagrams

Size Variations

	Twin	Full/Queen	King
Finished Size	65" x 85"	85" x 90"	95" x 95"
Number of Blocks	165	240	289
Blocks Set	11 x 15	15 x 16	17 x 17

Materials for Size Variations

		Twin	Full/Queen	King
	Fabric A	3⅞ yards	5⅜ yards	6½ yards
	Fabric B	3⅞ yards	5⅜ yards	6½ yards
	Fabric C	2⅜ yards	2½ yards	2⅝ yards
	Binding fabric	¾ yard	¾ yard	¾ yard
	Backing fabric	5¼ yards	5½ yards	8¾ yards

Little Cedar Tree by Marsha McCloskey, Seattle, Washington, 1995.
Machine-quilted by Barbara Ford.

Prairie Queen

In her 1929 book *Old Patchwork Quilts,* Ruth Finley included Prairie Queen among

the "simple but widely used nine-patches that every person interested in quilts should know."

I chose the pattern because it's ideal for rotary cutting and strip piecing.

I mixed five blue fabrics in prints and plaids of varying intensities. The crisp, clean result reminds me

of country French peasant costumes—simple and lively.

Approximate finished size: 68" x 80"* • Blocks: 20 (9") blocks

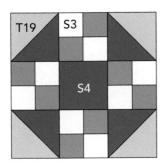

Materials

	Fabric A (light blue small plaid)	¾ yard
	Fabric B (medium blue print)	¾ yard
	Fabric C (light blue print)	1⅝ yards
	Fabric D (dark blue print)	1⅝ yards
	Fabric E (blue large plaid)	3 yards
	Binding fabric	¾ yard
	Backing fabric	4¼ yards
	Precut batting	72" x 90"

This quilt fits a twin bed. Requirements for other sizes are listed on page 74.

Cutting

Instructions are for rotary cutting. To check cutting accuracy, compare rotary-cut pieces to patterns S3, S4, and T19 (see pattern index, page 146). For traditional piecing, use these patterns to make templates.

Note: Cut all strips lengthwise.

From Fabric A (light plaid), cut:
• 18 (2" x 27") strips for four-patches (S3).

From Fabric B (medium print), cut:
• 18 (2" x 27") strips for four-patches (S3).

From Fabric C (light print), cut:
• 10 (14") squares for triangle-squares (T19).

From Fabric D (dark print), cut:
• 10 (14") squares for triangle-squares (T19).
• 20 (3½") squares (S4).

From Fabric E (large plaid), cut:
• 4 (6" x 75") strips for borders.
• 5 (3½" x 95") strips. From these, cut 49 (3½" x 9½") pieces for lattice.

Strip-Piecing Four-Patches

1. With right sides facing, join 1 strip of Fabric A and 1 strip of Fabric B, stitching on 1 long side. Repeat to make 18 strip sets. Press seam allowances toward darker fabric.

2. With right sides facing, match 2 strip sets so that each fabric faces the other and opposing seam allowances are nested. Rotary-cut 2"-wide segments from nested strips *(Diagram A).* Each pair of strips yields 13 units.

3. Join each pair of cut units to make 1 four-patch *(Diagram B).* Repeat to make a total of 110 four-patches, 80 for blocks and 30 for cornerstones.

(continued)

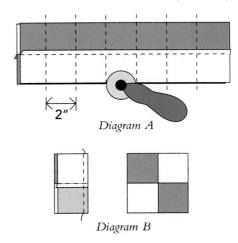

Diagram A

Diagram B

Bias-Strip Piecing Triangle-Squares

See page 16 for detailed instructions on bias-strip piecing two-triangle squares.

1. With right sides facing, match 1 (14") square of Fabric C with 1 (14") square of Fabric D.

2. Cutting through both layers, cut the squares diagonally from corner to corner to establish true bias (a 45° angle). Measuring from each bias edge, cut 3¼"-wide strips *(Diagram C)*. You'll get 4 sets of strips and 2 sets of leftover corner triangles.

3. Join each pair of strips along 1 long edge; then join pairs to complete a bias-strip setup as shown *(Diagram D)*. Press seam allowances toward darker fabric. Using a square ruler with bias marking, rotary-cut 16 (3½") two-triangle squares from this setup (2 from corners, 14 from strips).

4. Repeat steps 1–3 with 9 remaining sets of 14" squares to get a total of 160 two-triangle squares. Set aside 80 units for blocks and 80 for sawtooth border.

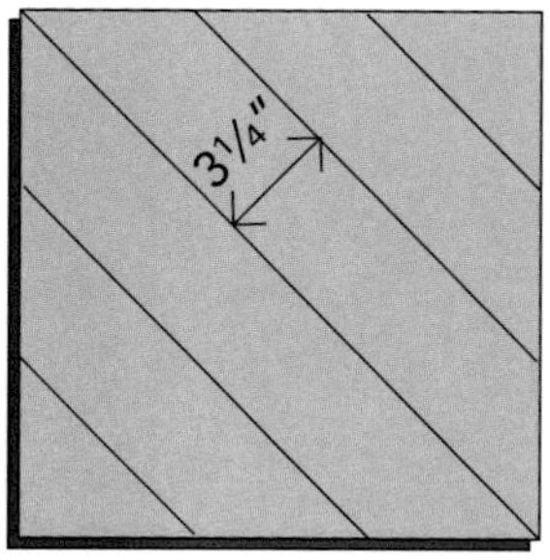

Diagram C

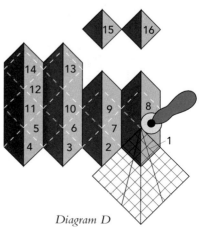

Diagram D

Making Blocks

1. For each block, select 1 (3½") square of Fabric D, 4 two-triangle squares, and 4 four-patches.

2. Join units in 3 horizontal rows *(Block Assembly Diagram)*. Press seam allowances away from four-patches. Then join rows to complete block.

3. Repeat to make a total of 20 blocks.

Quilt Assembly

1. For each lattice row, join 4 lattice strips and 5 cornerstones as shown

(Row Assembly Diagram). Press seam allowances toward lattice strips. Make 6 lattice rows.

Block Assembly Diagram

Row Assembly Diagram

Size Variations

	Full	Queen	King
Finished Size	80" x 92"	92" x 92"	104" x 104"
Number of Blocks	30	36	49
Blocks Set	5 x 6	6 x 6	7 x 7
Number of Four-Patches	162	193	260
Number of Triangle-Squares	216	248	316
Number of Lattice Strips	71	84	112

Materials for Size Variations

Fabric A	1 yard	1⅛ yards	1½ yards
Fabric B	1 yard	1⅛ yards	1½ yards
Fabric C	2⅛ yards	2½ yards	3 yards
Fabric D	2⅛ yards	2½ yards	3 yards
Fabric E	3 yards	3½ yards	4⅜ yards
Binding	¾ yard	¾ yard	1 yard
Backing	5¾ yards	8½ yards	9½ yards

2. For each block row, join 4 blocks and 5 lattice strips as shown. Press seam allowances toward lattice strips. Make 5 block rows.

3. Referring to photo for placement, join rows. Press seam allowances toward lattice rows.

Adding Borders

1. Use remaining two-triangle squares to make sawtooth border. For each side border, join 21 squares in a vertical row, always sewing light triangle to dark triangle (see photo). Join borders to quilt sides, easing to fit as needed. For top and bottom borders, join 19 squares in each horizontal row. (Note that 1 triangle is turned at end of each row; see photo.) Add borders to top and bottom edges.

2. Referring to instructions on page 20, measure quilt from top to bottom; then trim 2 border strips to match length. Join borders to quilt sides. Press seam allowances toward borders.

3. Measure quilt from side to side; then trim remaining borders to match quilt width. Join borders to top and bottom edges. Press seam allowances toward borders.

Finishing

1. Mark quilting design on quilt top as desired. Quilt shown is quilted in-the-ditch with an X quilted through each four-patch and a wavy cable quilted in borders and lattice strips. Two other quilting suggestions are shown here *(Alternate Quilting Diagrams).*

2. Divide backing fabric into 2 (2⅛-yard) lengths; then join lengths to make 1 (76" x 88") backing. Layer backing, batting, and quilt top (backing seam will run parallel to top and bottom edges of quilt top). Baste. Quilt as marked or as desired.

3. Cut 9 yards of 1½"-wide bias binding. See page 26 for instructions on making and applying binding.

Prairie Queen by Marsha McCloskey, Seattle, Washington, 1994. Machine-quilted by Barbara Ford.

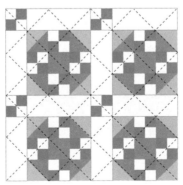 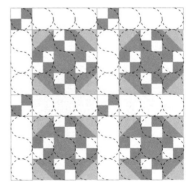

Alternate Quilting Diagrams

Chimney Sweep

Carole Collins, who teaches a class called "Getting the Antique Look," blended 35 prints to create this simple but striking quilt. Each block is a different fabric mix. To get an authentic look, Carole deliberately avoided smooth turns at the corners of the sawtooth border—each one is different! A brick red print for set pieces and borders pulls it all together.

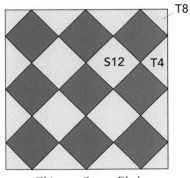

Chimney Sweep Block

Materials

	Fabric A (assorted light prints)	3 yards total
	Fabric B (assorted dark prints)	2½ yards total
	Fabric C (brick red)	4⅞ yards
	Binding	¾ yard
	Backing fabric	7½ yards
	Precut batting	90" x 108"

* This quilt fits a full or queen-size bed. Requirements for other sizes are listed below.

Cutting

Instructions are for rotary cutting. To check cutting accuracy, compare rotary-cut pieces to patterns T4, T8, and S12 (see pattern index, page 146). For traditional piecing, use these patterns to make templates.

From Fabric A (light prints), cut:
• 100 (3") squares (S12), 4 for each block.
• 50 (4¹³⁄₁₆") squares. Cut each square in quarters diagonally to get 200 quarter-square triangles (T4), 8 for each block.
• 50 (2⅝") squares. Cut each square in half diagonally to get 100 half-square triangles (T8), 4 for each block.
• 16 (8") squares for sawtooth border.

From Fabric B (dark prints), cut:
• 225 (3") squares (S12), 9 for each block.
• 16 (8") squares for sawtooth border.

From Fabric C (brick red), cut:
• 4 (3" x 88") lengthwise strips for outer border.
• 16 (11") squares for set squares.
• 4 (16¼") squares. Cut each square in quarters diagonally to get 16 quarter-square triangles for side set triangles.
• 2 (8⅜") squares. Cut each square in half diagonally to get 4 half-square triangles for corner set triangles.

Making Blocks

1. For each block, select 4 squares, 8 T4 triangles, and 4 T8 triangles of 1 light fabric; then choose 9 matching Fabric B squares.
2. Join light and dark squares in diagonal rows *(Block Assembly Diagram)*. Add triangles to row ends as shown. Press seam allowances toward dark squares.
3. Join rows to complete block. Repeat to make a total of 25 blocks.

(continued)

Block Assembly Diagram

Size Variations

	Crib	Twin	King
Finished Size	40" x 55"	70" x 85"	99½" x 99½"
Number of Blocks	6	20	36
Blocks Set	2 x 3	4 x 5	6 x 6
Number of Set Squares	3	12	25
Number of Side Set Triangles	6	14	20
Number of Triangle-Squares for Sawtooth Border	64	112	148

Materials for Size Variations

		Crib	Twin	King
	Fabric A	1⅛ yards	2¼ yards	3⅝ yards
	Fabric B	1 yard	1⅞ yards	3⅛ yards
	Fabric C	2 yards	2⅞ yards	4⅝ yards
	Binding	½ yard	⅝ yard	¾ yard
	Backing	1¾ yards	5¼ yards	9 yards

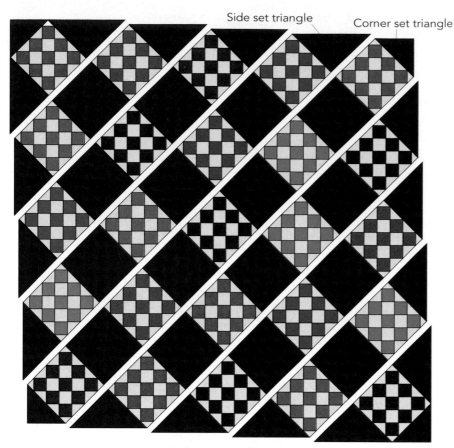

Side set triangle

Corner set triangle

Quilt Assembly Diagram

of 3"-wide strips and 2 sets of leftover corner triangles *(Diagram A)*.

3. Join each pair of bias strips; then join pairs to complete a bias-strip setup as shown *(Diagram B)*. Press seam allowances toward dark fabric.

4. Using a square ruler with bias marking, rotary-cut 7 (3") squares from this setup, 2 from corners and 5 from strips *(Diagram B)*.

5. To get an eighth triangle-square out of this setup, join remaining edge pieces *(Diagram C)* and cut 1 more square.

6. Repeat with remaining sets of A and B squares to make a total of 124 two-triangle squares.

Adding Borders

1. For each side border, join 30 triangle-squares in a vertical row, sewing light fabrics to dark fabrics (see photo). Join borders to quilt sides. (See page 20 for tips on working with pieced borders.)

2. For top and bottom borders, join 32 triangle-squares in each horizontal row. Join borders to quilt.

3. Referring to instructions on page 20, measure quilt from top to bottom; then trim 2 Fabric C border strips to match length. Join borders to quilt sides. Press seam allowances toward borders.

4. Measure quilt from side to side; then trim remaining borders to match quilt width. Join borders to top and bottom edges. Press seam allowances toward borders.

Quilt Assembly

To assemble this quilt, blocks are set on point, alternating with set pieces.

1. Lay out Chimney Sweep blocks in diagonal rows, alternating blocks with set squares *(Quilt Assembly Diagram)*. Position a set triangle at ends of each row as shown. Arrange blocks to get a pleasing balance of color and contrast.

2. Join blocks and set pieces in rows as shown. Press seam allowances toward set pieces. Then join rows.

Bias-Strip Piecing Triangle-Squares for Sawtooth Border

See page 16 for detailed instructions on bias-strip piecing two-triangle squares.

1. With right sides facing, match 8" squares of fabrics A and B.

2. Cutting through both layers, cut squares diagonally from corner to corner to establish true bias (a 45° angle). Measuring from cut edges, cut 2 sets

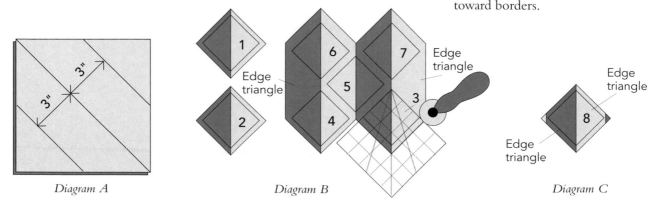

Diagram A

Edge triangle

Edge triangle

Edge triangle

Diagram B

Edge triangle

Edge triangle

Diagram C

Chimney Sweep by Carole Collins, Norfolk, Nebraska, 1994.

Finishing

1. Mark quilting design on quilt top as desired. Quilt shown is quilted with diagonal lines that cross in an X through squares of each block and straight lines in set pieces. Diagonal lines of quilting follow triangle-square seams and extend into outer border. Two other quilting suggestions are shown here *(Alternate Quilting Diagrams)*.

2. Divide backing fabric into 3 (2½–yard) lengths. Cut 1 length in half lengthwise and discard 1 half. Join remaining 3 panels, sewing 2 wide panels to sides of narrow panel. Layer backing, batting, and quilt top. Baste. Quilt as marked or as desired.

3. Cut 10 yards of 1½"-wide bias binding. See page 26 for instructions on making and applying binding.

 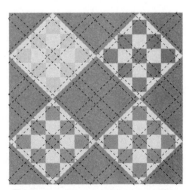

Alternate Quilting Diagrams

Indiana Puzzle

The word "Puzzle" is a clue to keep your wits about you when piecing. Mind the placement of light and dark in these blocks, as it's easy to get swirls going the wrong way. Making this scrap quilt was fun because it has some favorite fabrics and colors that make me happy. I used as many prints as I could, trying not to repeat any fabric in the same block. With so many choices to make, piecing is never tedious.

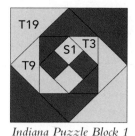

Indiana Puzzle Block 1

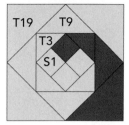

Indiana Puzzle Block 2

Approximate finished size: 78" x 90" • Blocks: 49 (6") blocks

Materials

■	Fabric A (assorted brown prints)	3 yards total
■	Fabric B (assorted light pink prints)	4¼ yards total
	Fabric C (light print for borders)	2⅜ yards
	Binding fabric	¾ yard
	Backing fabric	5½ yards
	Precut batting	81" x 96"

* This quilt fits a full bed. Requirements for other sizes are listed on page 82.

Cutting

Instructions are for rotary cutting. To check cutting accuracy, compare rotary-cut pieces to patterns S1, S15, T3, T9, and T19 (see pattern index, page 146). For traditional piecing, use these patterns to make templates.

From Fabric A (brown prints), cut:
• 12 (9") squares for bias-strip piecing sawtooth border.
• 20 (6½") squares (S15) for alternate set squares.
• 40 (3⅞") squares. Cut each square in half diagonally to get 80 half-square triangles (T19).
• 40 (3") squares. Cut each square in half diagonally to get 80 half-square triangles (T9).
• 40 (2⅜") squares. Cut each square in half diagonally to get 80 half-square triangles (T3).
• 80 (1⅞₆") squares (S1).

From Fabric B (pink prints), cut:
• 4 (3½" x 72") lengthwise strips for inner borders. (Piece random lengths to get needed length.)
• 30 (6½") squares (S15) for alternate set squares.
• 58 (3⅞") squares. Cut each square in half diagonally to get 116 half-square triangles (T19).

• 58 (3") squares. Cut each square in half diagonally to get 116 half-square triangles (T9).
• 58 (2⅜") squares. Cut each square in half diagonally to get 116 half-square triangles (T3).
• 116 (1⅞₆") squares (S1).
• 12 (9") squares for sawtooth border.

From Fabric C (light print), cut:
• 4 (6½" x 83") lengthwise strips for outer borders.

Making Blocks

There are two pieced blocks in this quilt that create a swirl when joined with alternating plain squares. Block 1 has pink and brown fabrics on opposite sides of the block. Block 2, which is placed around the outside edge of the patchwork, has brown on just one side of the block.

1. For each Block 1, select 2 S1 squares and 2 each of triangles T3, T9, and T19 from Fabric A. Select same pieces of Fabric B.

2. Join squares in pairs; then join pairs to make a four-patch *(Diagram A)*.

3. Sew T3 triangles of Fabric B to opposite sides of four-patch *(Diagram B)*. Press seam allowances toward triangles. Then sew Fabric A triangles to remaining sides.

4. In same manner, add T9 triangles *(Diagram C)* and T19 triangles *(Diagram D)* to complete 1 block.

5. Repeat to make a total of 31 of Block 1. Make 18 of Block 2 in same manner, following *Block Diagram* for color placement. *(continued)*

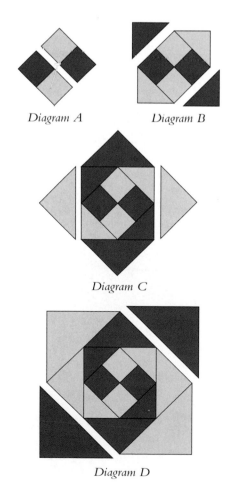

Diagram A   *Diagram B*

Diagram C

Diagram D

Quilt Assembly

Refer to *Row Assembly Diagram* carefully to be sure positions of blocks and set squares are correct in each row. Lay out all rows to be sure blocks spin in the right direction before you sew.

1. For Row 1, join 4 of Block 2 and 5 S15 squares of Fabric B as shown. Make 2 of Row 1.

2. For Row 2, join 3 of Block 1, 4 S15 squares of Fabric A, and 2 of Block 2 (at row ends) as shown. Make 5 of Row 2.

3. For Row 3, join 4 of Block 1 and 5 S15 squares of Fabric B. Make 4 of Row 3.

4. Join rows 1, 2, and 3 as shown in *Row Assembly Diagram*. Referring to photo, continue joining rows, alternating rows 2 and 3. Add remaining Row 1 as last row.

Bias-Strip Piecing Triangle-Squares for Sawtooth Border

See page 16 for more instructions on bias-strip piecing two-triangle squares.

1. With right sides facing, match 9" squares of fabrics A and B.

2. Cutting through both layers, cut squares diagonally from corner to corner to establish true bias (45° angle). Measuring from cut edges, cut 2 sets of 3¼"-wide strips and 2 sets of leftover corner triangles *(Diagram E)*.

3. Join each pair of bias strips; then join pairs to complete a bias-strip setup as shown *(Diagram F)*. Press seam allowances toward dark fabric.

4. Using a square ruler with bias marking, rotary-cut 7 (3½") squares from this setup, 2 from corners and 5 from strips *(Diagram F)*.

5. To get an eighth triangle-square, join remaining edge triangles *(Diagram G)* and cut 1 more square.

6. Repeat with remaining sets of A and B squares to make a total of 92 two-triangle squares (and 4 extra).

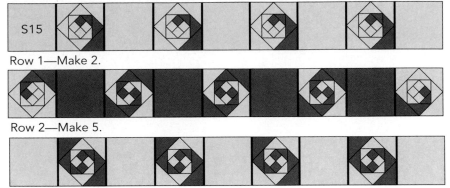

Row 1—Make 2.

Row 2—Make 5.

Row 3—Make 4.

Row Assembly Diagram

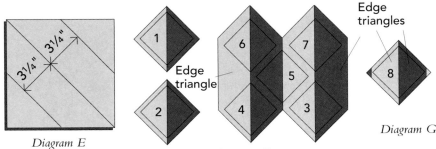

Diagram E

Edge triangle

Diagram F

Edge triangles

Diagram G

Size Variations

	Twin	Queen	King
Finished Size	66" x 90"	90" x 90"	102" x 102"
Number of Block 1	22	40	60
Number of Block 2	16	20	24
Number of A Set Squares	15	25	36
Number of B Set Squares	24	36	49
Triangle-Squares for Sawtooth Border	84	100	116

Materials for Size Variations

		Twin	Queen	King
	Fabric A	2½ yards	3½ yards	4½ yards
	Fabric B	3¾ yards	5 yards	5¾ yards
	Fabric C	2⅜ yards	2¾ yards	3 yards
	Binding fabric	⅝ yard	¾ yard	¾ yard
	Backing fabric	5½ yards	8¼ yards	9⅜ yards

Adding Borders

1. Referring to instructions on page 20, measure quilt from top to bottom; then trim 2 (3½"-wide) borders to match length. Join borders to quilt sides. Press seam allowances toward borders.

2. Measure quilt from side to side; then trim remaining 3½"-wide borders to match. Join borders to top and bottom edges of quilt. Press seam allowances toward borders.

3. Referring to photo, join 24 triangle-squares to make 1 side sawtooth border. When joining squares, sew dark triangles to light triangles except in middle of strip where triangles switch directions. Repeat to make second side border. Join borders to quilt sides, easing to fit as necessary.

4. Join 22 triangle-squares as shown to make sawtooth border for top edge. Note how units at strip ends are turned. Repeat to make bottom border. Join borders to top and bottom edges of quilt. Press seam allowances toward inner border.

5. Repeat steps 1 and 2 to join outer borders.

Finishing

1. Mark quilting design on quilt top as desired. On quilt shown, patchwork is outline-quilted and set squares have a stylized X quilted across seam lines. Two other quilting suggestions are shown here *(Alternate Quilting Diagrams)*.

2. Divide backing into 2 equal lengths. Join lengths to assemble backing. Layer backing, batting, and quilt top. Baste. Quilt as marked or as desired.

3. Cut 10 yards of 1½"-wide bias binding. See page 26 for instructions on making and applying binding.

Indiana Puzzle by Marsha McCloskey, Seattle, Washington, 1995. Machine-quilted by Barbara Ford.

 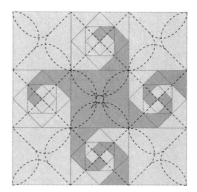

Alternate Quilting Diagrams

English Wedding Ring

Several design elements give this quilt the style of an antique. First, Carole Collins used shirting prints (15 fat quarters) for light background fabrics. And, since many antique quilts lack borders, Carole didn't put a border on this quilt. Finally, she used thin cotton batting to get an authentic flat look. The patchwork is quick and easy if you use the bias-strip method for making two-triangle squares.

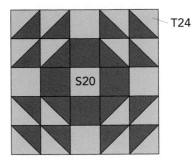

English Wedding Ring Block

Materials

	Fabric A (assorted light prints)	3¼ yards total
	Fabric B (assorted dark prints)	3 yards total
	Fabric C (navy print)	3¼ yards
	Binding fabric	¾ yard
	Backing fabric	5¼ yards
	Precut batting	72" x 90"

* This quilt fits a twin bed. Requirements for other sizes are on page 86.

Cutting

Instructions are for rotary cutting. To check cutting accuracy, compare rotary-cut pieces to patterns S20 and T24 (see pattern index, page 146). For traditional piecing, use these patterns to make templates.

Fat quarters are ideal for this scrappy quilt, as you can cut pieces for 2 blocks from each fat quarter.

From Fabric A (light prints), cut:
• 30 (10") squares for bias-strip piecing, 1 for each block.
• 150 (2½") squares (S20), 5 for each block.

From Fabric B (dark prints), cut:
• 30 (10") squares for bias-strip piecing, 1 for each block.
• 120 (2½") squares (S20), 4 for each block.

From Fabric C (navy print), cut:
• 5 (15⅜") squares. Cut each square in quarters diagonally to get 18 side set triangles (and 2 extra).
• 20 (10½") squares for set squares.
• 2 (8") squares. Cut each square in half diagonally to get 4 corner set triangles.

Bias-Strip Piecing Triangle-Squares

See page 16 for detailed instructions on bias-strip piecing two-triangle squares.

1. With right sides facing, match 1 (10") square of Fabric A with a Fabric B square.

2. Cutting through both layers, cut squares diagonally from corner to corner to establish true bias (45° angle). Measuring from cut edges, cut 4 sets of 2½"-wide bias strips and 2 sets of leftover corner triangles *(Diagram A)*.

3. Join each pair of bias strips; then join pairs to complete a bias-strip setup as shown *(Diagram B)*. Press seam allowances toward dark fabric.

4. Using a square ruler with bias marking, rotary-cut 16 (2½") triangle-squares from this setup.

5. Repeat with remaining A and B squares, making 16 triangle-squares for each block.

Making Blocks

1. For 1 block, select matching sets of 16 triangle-squares, 5 Fabric A squares, and 4 Fabric B squares. All squares should be same size.

2. Join units in 5 vertical rows, positioning light and dark fabrics as shown *(Block Assembly Diagram)*.

3. Join rows to complete block.

4. Repeat to make a total of 30 blocks.

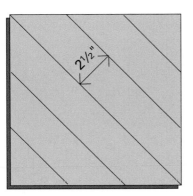

Diagram A

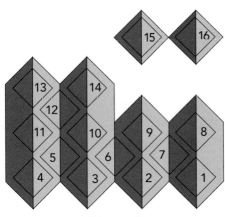

Diagram B

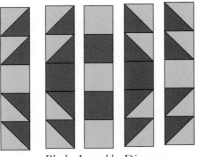

Block Assembly Diagram

(continued)

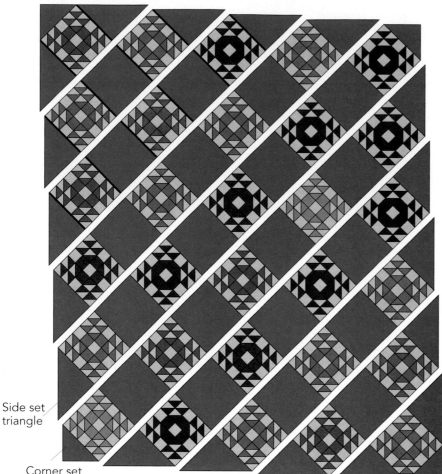

Side set
triangle

Corner set
triangle

Quilt Assembly Diagram

Quilt Assembly

To assemble this quilt, blocks are set on the diagonal, alternating with square set pieces. Set triangles fill in around the edge of the quilt.

1. Lay out blocks in diagonal rows, alternating blocks with set squares *(Quilt Assembly Diagram)*. Position a set triangle at ends of each row as shown. Arrange blocks to achieve a pleasing balance of color and contrast.

2. Join blocks and set pieces in diagonal rows as shown. Press seam allowances toward set pieces. Join rows.

Finishing

1. Mark quilting design on quilt top as desired. Quilt shown is hand-quilted in Baptist Fan design. Pattern and instructions to mark design are on page 23. Two other quilting suggestions are shown here *(Alternate Quilting Diagrams)*.

2. Divide backing fabric into 2 (2⅝-yard) lengths. Join lengths to make backing. Layer backing, batting, and quilt top. Baste. Quilt as marked or as desired.

3. Cut 10 yards of 1½"-wide bias binding. See page 26 to instructions on making and applying binding.

Size Variations

	Crib	Full/Queen	King
Finished Size	43" x 43"	86" x 101"	101" x 101"
Number of Blocks	9	42	49
Blocks Set	3 x 3	6 x 7	7 x 7
Number of Set Squares	4	30	36
Number of Side Set Triangles	8	22	24

Materials for Size Variations

		Crib	Full/Queen	King
	Fabric A	1⅛ yards	4¼ yards	5 yards
	Fabric B	1⅛ yards	4⅛ yards	5 yards
	Fabric C	1 yard	3½ yards	4 yards
	Binding fabric	½ yard	¾ yard	¾ yard
	Backing fabric	1⅜ yards	6 yards	9 yards

Alternate Quilting Diagrams

English Wedding Ring by Carole Collins, Norfolk, Nebraska, 1994.

Lost Ships

In colonial times, when fabric was scarce and expensive, lucky wives sometimes received a yard of chintz from a thoughtful husband. In keeping with this tradition, this quilt uses 1 yard of chintz decorator fabric for the large triangles. When I ran out of the lemon yellow chintz, I simply stopped making blocks and declared the quilt top finished.

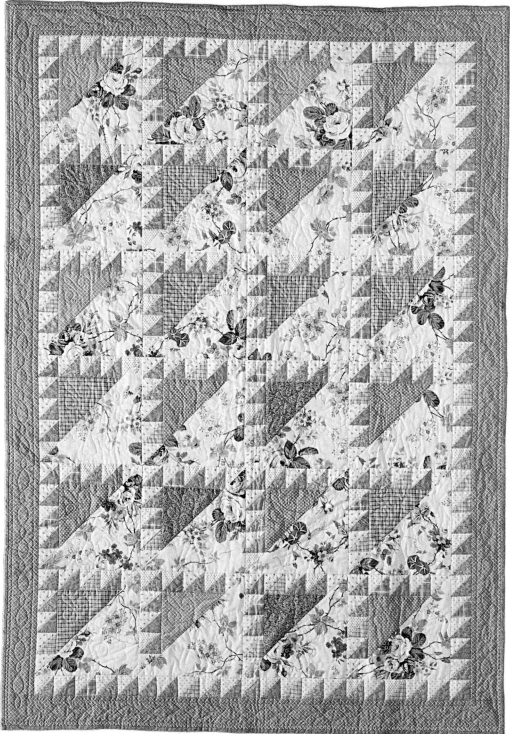

Lost Ships by Marsha McCloskey, Seattle, Washington, 1995.
Machine-quilted by Barbara Ford.

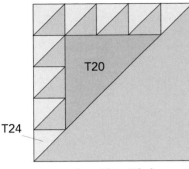

Lost Ships Block

Materials

	Fabric A (yellow chintz)	1 yard
	Fabric B (assorted light prints)	2 yards total
	Fabric C (assorted green prints)	2 yards total
	Fabric D (assorted pink prints, includes binding)	2 yards total
	Backing fabric	3 yards
	Precut batting	72" x 90"

* This quilt is a crib size or wall hanging. Requirements for other sizes are listed on page 90.

Cutting

Instructions are for rotary cutting. To check cutting accuracy, compare rotary-cut pieces to patterns T20 and T24 (see pattern index, page 146). For traditional piecing, use these patterns to make templates.

From Fabric A (yellow chintz), cut:
• 12 (10⅞") squares. Cut each square in half diagonally to get 24 half-square triangles. For easy matching, trim points at 10½" (see page 13).

From Fabric B (light prints), cut:
• 14 (10") squares for bias-strip piecing.
• 24 (2⅞") squares. Cut each square in half diagonally to get 48 half-square triangles (T24), 2 for each block. Trim points at 2½".

From Fabric C (green prints), cut:
• 14 (10") squares for bias-strip piecing.

From Fabric D (pink prints), cut:
• 4 (3½" x 65") lengthwise strips for outer border.
• 1 (28" x 42") rectangle for binding.
• 12 (6⅞") squares. Cut each square in half diagonally to get 24 half-square triangles (T20), 1 for each block. Trim points at 6½".

Bias-Strip Piecing Triangle-Squares

See page 16 for more instructions on bias-strip piecing two-triangle squares.
1. With right sides facing, match 1 (10") square of Fabric B with a Fabric C square.
2. Cutting through both layers, cut squares diagonally from corner to corner to establish true bias (45° angle). Measuring from cut edges, cut 4 sets of 2½"-wide bias strips and 2 sets of leftover corner triangles *(Diagram A)*.
3. Join each pair of bias strips; then join pairs to complete a bias-strip setup as shown *(Diagram B)*. Join corner triangles. Press seam allowances toward darker fabric.
4. Using a square ruler with bias marking, rotary-cut 16 (2½") squares from this setup.
5. Repeat with remaining B and C squares to make a total of 219 two-triangle squares, 7 for each block and 51 for sawtooth border.

Making Blocks

1. For each block, select 7 triangle-squares, 2 Fabric B triangles, 1 Fabric D triangle, and 1 Fabric A triangle.
2. Join 3 triangle-squares in a vertical row and 4 triangle-squares in a horizontal row as shown *(Block Assembly Diagram)*. Join T24 triangles to row ends as shown. *(continued)*

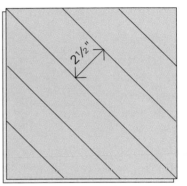

Diagram A

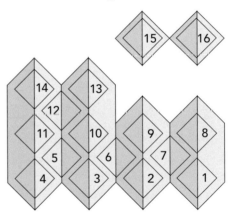

Diagram B

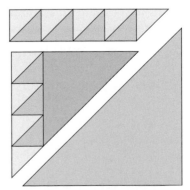

Block Assembly Diagram

3. Join 3-square row to side of T20 triangle. Then join 4-square row to top edge as shown.

4. Sew pieced unit to Fabric A triangle to complete block. Repeat to make a total of 24 blocks.

Quilt Assembly

1. Lay out blocks in 6 horizontal rows, with 4 blocks in each row *(Row Assembly Diagram)*. Join blocks in rows.

2. To complete each row, join 5 triangle-squares in a vertical row and sew unit to right edge of row.

3. Join rows as shown.

Adding Borders

1. Referring to photo on page 88, join remaining 21 triangle-squares in a row. Sew row to bottom edge of quilt to complete sawtooth border.

2. Referring to instructions on page 20, measure quilt from top to bottom; then trim 2 Fabric D border strips to match length. Join borders to quilt sides. Press seam allowances toward borders.

3. Measure quilt from side to side; then trim remaining borders to match. Join borders to top and bottom edges of quilt.

Finishing

1. Mark quilting design on quilt top as desired. Quilt shown has in-the-ditch quilting around small triangles and a chain quilted in border. I used a purchased stencil to mark a fleur-de-lis motif in chintz triangles (look for a similar stencil at your quilt shop). Two other quilting suggestions are shown here *(Alternate Quilting Diagrams)*.

2. Divide backing into 2 (1½-yard) lengths. Join lengths to assemble backing. Layer backing, batting, and quilt top. Baste. Quilt as marked or as desired.

3. Cut 7 yards of 1½"-wide bias binding. See page 26 for instructions on making and applying binding.

Size Variations

	Twin	Full/Queen	King
Finished Size	68" x 88"	88" x 88"	98" x 98"
Number of Blocks	48	64	81
Blocks Set	6 x 8	8 x 8	9 x 9
Number of Triangle-Squares (includes border)	407	529	658

Materials for Size Variations

		Twin	Full/Queen	King
	Fabric A	2 yards	2½ yards	3½ yards
	Fabric B	2½ yards	3 yards	3⅝ yards
	Fabric C	2¼ yards	2¾ yards	3¼ yards
	Fabric D	2½ yards	2⅝ yards	3 yards
	Backing fabric	4¼ yards	8 yards	9 yards

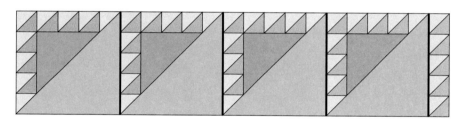

Row Assembly Diagram

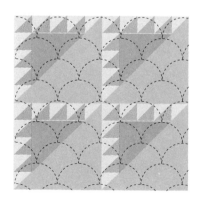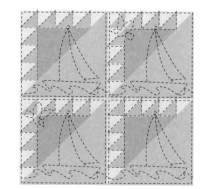

Alternate Quilting Diagrams

Cleo's Basket

This is such a cheerful quilt! Use scraps from your fabric collection or buy fat-quarters to get a nice variety of prints. For this red quilt, Cleo Nollette chose 21 light and 21 dark prints. She cut enough of each print for two blocks and then mixed the pieces to get a scrappy look. Any two-color combination will give you the traditional look of this quilt—try green and white or yellow and blue.

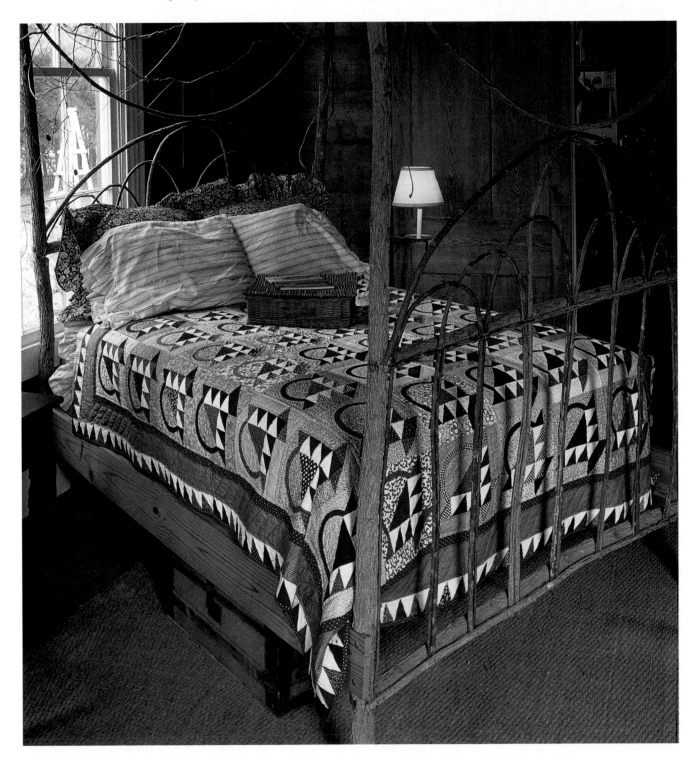

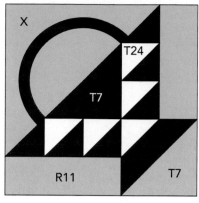

Basket Block

Materials

▨	Fabric A (assorted light/medium red prints)	4½ yards total
▮	Fabric B (assorted dark red prints)	4¼ yards total
▯	Fabric C (assorted white prints)	2 yards total
	Binding fabric	⅝ yard
	Backing fabric	5 yards
	Precut batting	72" x 90"
	½"-wide bias pressing bar	
	Template plastic	

* This quilt fits a twin bed. Requirements for other sizes are on page 95.

Cutting

Instructions are for rotary cutting. To check cutting accuracy, compare rotary-cut pieces to patterns S20, T7, T24, and R11 (see pattern index, page 146). For traditional piecing, use these patterns to make templates.

From Fabric A (light red), cut:
- 4 (4" x 76") lengthwise strips for middle border.
- 21 (8⅞") squares. Cut each square in half diagonally to get 42 of Triangle X, 1 for each block.
- 21 (4⅞") squares. Cut each square in half diagonally to get 42 half-square triangles (T7), 1 for each block.
- 84 (2½" x 6½") rectangles (R11), 2 for each block.

From Fabric B (dark red), cut:
- 8 (1¼"-wide) crosswise strips for inner border.
- 23 (10") squares for bias-strip piecing.
- 21 (9") squares. Set these aside for basket handles and T7 triangles.
- 84 (2⅞") squares. Cut each square in half diagonally to get 168 half-square triangles (T24), 4 for each block.
- 2 (2½") squares for sawtooth border corners (S20).

From Fabric C (white), cut:
- 23 (10") squares for bias-strip piecing.

Bias-Strip Piecing Triangle-Squares

See page 16 for detailed instructions on bias-strip piecing two-triangle squares.

1. With right sides facing, match 1 (10") square of Fabric B with a 10" Fabric C square.

2. Cutting through both layers, cut squares diagonally from corner to corner to establish true bias (45° angle). Measuring from cut edges, cut 4 sets of 2½"-wide bias strips and 2 sets of corner triangles *(Diagram A)*.

3. Join each pair of bias strips; then join pairs to complete a bias-strip setup as shown *(Diagram B)*. Join corner triangles. Press seam allowances toward darker fabric.

4. Using a square ruler with bias marking, rotary-cut 16 (2½") squares from this setup.

5. Repeat with remaining B and C squares to make a total of 354 two-triangle squares—5 for each block, 146 for sawtooth border, and 12 extra.

Diagram A

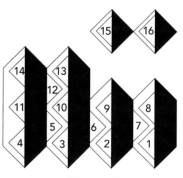

Diagram B

Making Handles for Baskets

1. Select 1 (9") square of Fabric B. Cut square in half diagonally to get 2 large triangles. Measuring from cut edge of 1 triangle, cut a 1½"-wide bias strip *(Photo 1)*. Cut another 1½"-wide bias strip from second triangle.

2. Cut a 1⅜"-wide bias strip from cut edge of each remaining triangle to get 2 T7 triangles *(Diagram C)*. Make sure each leg of this triangle measures 4⅞". Repeat with remaining 9" squares until you have a total of 42 (1½"-wide) bias strips and 42 T7 triangles, 1 for each block. Discard 1⅜"-wide strips.

3. With wrong sides facing and edges aligned, fold 1 bias strip in half lengthwise. Machine-stitch a scant ¼" from raw edge, making a narrow tube. Repeat with remaining strips.

4. Slide tube onto pressing bar *(Photo 2)*, with seam on flat side of bar. Press seam allowances to 1 side *(Photo 3)*. Handle metal bars with caution—they get hot! Remove bar; trim seam allowances if necessary. Repeat with remaining strips.

5. Make a template of Handle Pattern (page 95). Mark center on template as indicated on pattern.

6. To prevent stretching during appliqué, stay-stitch diagonal edge of each Triangle X, ⅛" from bias edge. Fold each triangle in half and lightly crease to mark center. Position template on right side of each triangle, aligning centers and bottom edges *(Diagram D)*. Use a lead pencil to lightly trace handle shape on triangle.

7. With seam against triangle fabric, baste or pin bias strip in place on triangle, using pencil markings as a guide. Bias should curve easily *(Photo 4)*, but a steam iron will help shape strip if necessary.

8. Appliqué handle in place by hand or topstitch edges by machine. Stitch inside curve first and then outside curve so bias will lie flat.

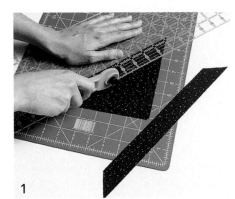

1

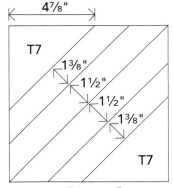

Diagram C

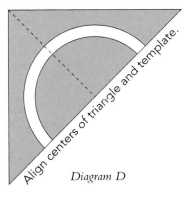

2

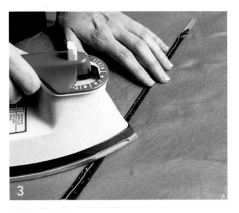

3

Align centers of triangle and template.

Diagram D

4

Making Blocks

1. For each block, select 5 triangle-squares, 4 T24 triangles, 2 R11 rectangles, 1 appliquéd Triangle X, and 1 T7 triangle *each* of fabrics A and B.

2. Join 2 triangle-squares in a vertical row and add a T24 triangle to top of row *(Block Assembly Diagram)*. Join this unit to 1 side of Fabric B T7 triangle as shown. Press seam allowances toward T7 triangle.

3. Join 3 more triangle-squares in a horizontal row, adding a T24 triangle to row end as shown. Join this unit to bottom of center unit. Press seam allowances toward T7.   *(continued)*

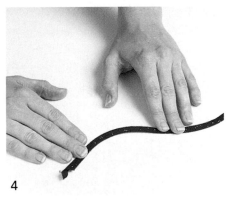

Block Assembly Diagram

4. Join T24 triangles to 1 end of each rectangle. Press seam allowances toward triangles. Then join these units to sides of center unit as shown.

5. Join Triangle X and remaining T7 triangle to complete block. Press seam allowances toward these triangles.

6. Repeat to make a total of 42 blocks.

Row Assembly Diagram

Quilt Assembly

1. Lay out blocks in 7 horizontal rows, with 6 blocks in each row *(Row Assembly Diagram).* Arrange blocks to achieve a pleasing balance of color and contrast.

2. Join blocks in rows. Then join rows.

Adding Borders

1. For inner border, join Fabric B strips end-to-end in pairs to make 4 border strips. Following instructions on page 20, measure quilt from top to bottom; then trim 2 border strips to match length. Join these borders to quilt sides. Measure quilt from side to side; then trim remaining strips to match. Join borders to top and bottom edges of quilt. Press seam allowances toward border.

2. Because middle border is a spacer between quilt center and sawtooth border, it is prudent to piece sawtooth border before adding middle border in order to make adjustments that might be necessary. See page 20 for more information about spacers.

3. Use remaining triangle-squares to assemble sawtooth border. For each side border, select 38 triangle-squares. Join triangle-squares in a vertical row, sewing light fabric to dark fabric. For top sawtooth border, select 34 triangle-squares. Join these in a horizontal row. Referring to photo, add 1 S20 square (Fabric B) to light triangle at end of row. Repeat for bottom border as shown.

4. Measure quilt from top to bottom, omitting seam allowances (approximately 71½"). Then measure length of pieced side border (approximately 76").

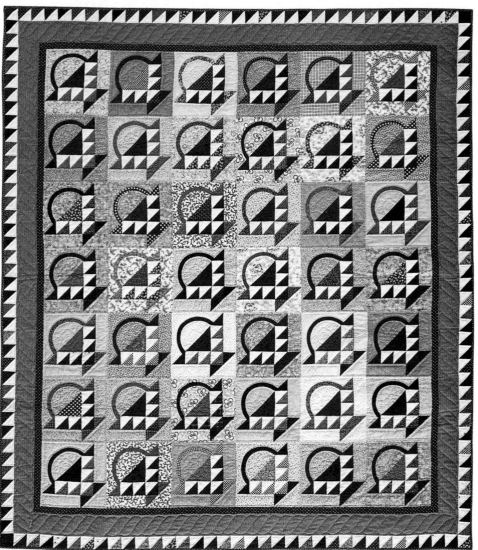

Cleo's Basket by Cleo Nollette, Seattle, Washington, 1995.
Quilt design by Marsha McCloskey.

Subtract to determine width of spacer border (76" - 71½" = 4½")—*finished* border width is half (4½" ÷ 2 = 2¼"), *plus* seam allowances (2¾"). Trim Fabric A border strips to appropriate width according to your own measurements. Repeat for top and bottom borders. If width of top and bottom borders differs slightly from side borders, it probably won't be noticeable.

5. When Fabric A border strips are trimmed to correct width, join borders to quilt as in Step 1.

6. Join side sawtooth borders to quilt sides, easing as necessary. Then join top and bottom borders.

Finishing

1. Mark quilting design on quilt top as desired. Quilt shown is outline-quilted, with a rose quilted below each basket handle and a feather chain in wide border. Two other quilting suggestions are shown here *(Alternate Quilting Diagrams)*.

2. Divide backing into 2 (2¾-yard) lengths. Join lengths to assemble backing. Layer backing, batting, and quilt top. Baste. Quilt as marked or as desired.

3. Cut 9⅛ yards of 1½"-wide bias binding. See page 26 for instructions on making and applying binding.

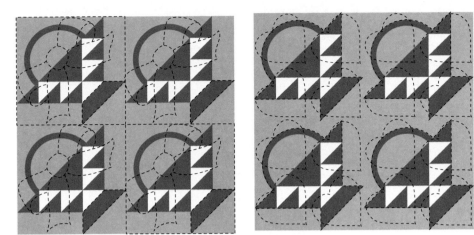

Alternate Quilting Diagrams

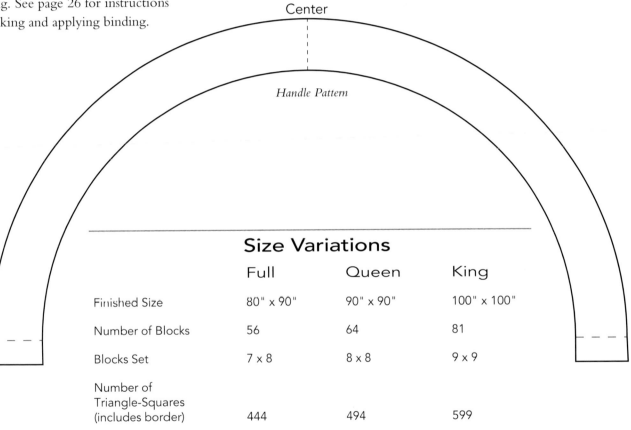

Center

Handle Pattern

Size Variations

	Full	Queen	King
Finished Size	80" x 90"	90" x 90"	100" x 100"
Number of Blocks	56	64	81
Blocks Set	7 x 8	8 x 8	9 x 9
Number of Triangle-Squares (includes border)	444	494	599

Materials for Size Variations

		Full	Queen	King
■	Fabric A	4¾ yards	5¼ yards	6¼ yards
■	Fabric B*	5 yards	5¾ yards	7 yards
□	Fabric C	2⅛ yards	2½ yards	3⅛ yards
	Binding fabric	¾ yard	¾ yard	¾ yard
	Backing fabric	5½ yards	8⅜ yards	9⅛ yards

* Border cut crosswise.

Ocean Waves

Old Ocean Waves quilts are often simple two-fabric treatments of blue or red with white. This quilt uses navy scraps, with a few pinks and greens mixed in for interest. I made the quilt over several years—it was my in-progress sample for classes. Over time, as I just grabbed random blue and white fabrics for the next class, the fabrics became a sampler of available prints and other quilts I was making.

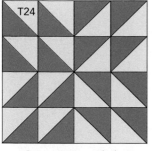

Ocean Waves Block 1

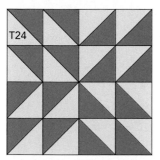

Ocean Waves Block 2

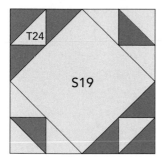

Ocean Waves Block 3

Cutting

Instructions are for rotary cutting. To check cutting accuracy, compare rotary-cut pieces to patterns S19, T7, T23, and T24 (see pattern index, page 146). For traditional piecing, use these patterns to make templates.

From Fabric A (navy prints), cut:
• 38 (10") squares for bias-strip piecing.
• 48 (2⅞") squares. Cut each square in half diagonally to get 96 half-square triangles (T24) for blocks. For easy matching, trim points at 2½" (see page 13).

Approximate finished size: 67" x 83"* • Blocks: 35 (8") blocks

Materials

	Fabric A (assorted navy prints)	3⅛ yards total
	Fabric B (assorted light prints)	4½ yards total
	Fabric C (green print)	½ yard
	Fabric D (navy stripe for borders, binding)	2⅛ yards
	Backing fabric	4 yards
	Precut batting	72" x 90"

* This quilt fits a twin bed. Requirements for other sizes are on page 100.

From Fabric B (light prints), cut:
• 4 (2½" x 68") lengthwise strips for inner border.
• 38 (10") squares for bias-strip piecing.
• 3 (9¼") squares. Cut each square in quarters diagonally to get 10 (and 2 extra) quarter-square triangles (T23) for Half Blocks 6 and 7.
• 48 (2⅞") squares. Cut each square in half diagonally to get 96 half-square triangles (T24). Trim points at 2½".
• 18 (6⅛") squares (S19) for Block 3.
• 2 (4⅞") squares. Cut each square in half diagonally to get 4 half-square triangles (T7) for Corner Blocks 8 and 9.

From Fabric C (green print), cut:
• 8 (1¼"-wide) crosswise strips for accent border.

From Fabric D (navy stripe), cut:
• 4 (5" x 76") lengthwise strips for outer border.
• 1 (20" x 35") piece for bias binding.

Diagram A

Bias-Strip Piecing Triangle-Squares

See page 16 for more instructions on bias-strip piecing two-triangle squares.

1. With right sides facing, match 1 (10") square of Fabric A with a Fabric B square.

2. Cutting through both layers, cut squares diagonally from corner to corner to establish true bias (45° angle). Measuring from cut edges, cut 4 sets of 2½"-wide bias strips and 2 sets of leftover corner triangles *(Diagram A)*.

3. Join each pair of bias strips; then join pairs to complete a bias-strip setup as shown *(Diagram B)*. Join corner triangles. Press seam allowances toward dark fabric.

4. Using a square ruler with bias marking, rotary-cut 16 (2½") squares from this setup.

5. Repeat with remaining A and B squares to make a total of 604 two-triangle squares, 480 for blocks and 124 for sawtooth border. *(continued)*

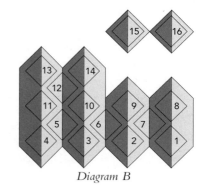

Diagram B

Making Blocks

I make this design with alternate blocks and half blocks to avoid set-in seams. There are three blocks and four half-blocks. Blocks 1 and 2 are made the same way, but placement of light and dark fabrics is reversed. Throughout construction of this quilt top, check position of dark and light patches carefully.

1. Select 16 triangle-squares for Block 1. For top row, join 2 triangle-squares, sewing light fabric to dark fabric *(Block 1 Assembly Diagram)*. Add 2 more triangle-squares to row ends to complete top row. Repeat for bottom row, positioning light and dark fabrics as shown. On wrong side, press seam allowances in both rows as shown in *Block 1 Pressing Diagram.*

2. For middle section of block, join triangle-squares in pairs vertically, matching light to dark as shown. Press seam allowances in opposite directions as shown *(Block 1 Pressing Diagram).* Join 2 pair to make center pinwheel. To avoid a lump in the center, press center seam open as shown. Then join remaining pairs to pinwheel sides to complete center section. Press as shown.

3. Join top and bottom rows to center section to complete block. Press joining seams away from center.

4. Repeat steps 1–3 to make 8 of Block 1. Make 9 of Block 2 in same manner, referring to *Block 2 Assembly Diagram* and *Block 2 Pressing Diagram.*

5. For Block 3, select 4 triangle-squares, 1 S19 square, 4 T24 triangles of Fabric A, and 4 T24 triangles of Fabric B. On 2 triangle-squares, join Fabric A triangles to both light sides of the square to make 2 triangular corner units *(Block 3 Assembly Diagram).* Join Fabric B triangles to remaining triangle-squares as shown. Press seam allowances away from triangle-squares.

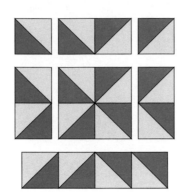

Block 1 Assembly Diagram—Make 8.

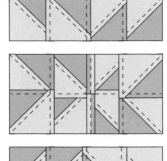

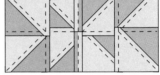

Block 1 Pressing Diagram

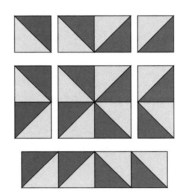

Block 2 Assembly Diagram—Make 9.

Block 2 Pressing Diagram

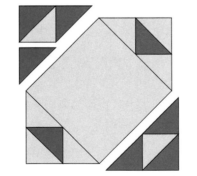

Block 3 Assembly Diagram—Make 18.

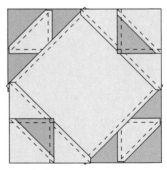

Block 3 Pressing Diagram

6. Join corner units to S19 square as shown to complete block. See *Block 3 Pressing Diagram* for pressing tips. Make 18 of Block 3.

7. For each of Half Block 4 and Half Block 5, select 8 triangle-squares. Join triangle-squares as shown *(Half Block Diagrams)*. Make 8 of Half Block 4 and 6 of Half Block 5.

8. For each of Half Block 6 and Half Block 7, select 2 triangle-squares, 1 T23 triangle, and 2 T24 triangles each of light and dark fabrics. For each Half Block, make 2 corner units as shown *(Half Block Diagrams)* and join units to large triangle. Make 4 of Half Block 6 and 6 of Half Block 7.

9. In same manner, make 2 of Corner Block 8 and 2 of Corner Block 9 *(Corner Block Diagrams)*.

Quilt Assembly

1. Lay out blocks in horizontal rows, with 7 blocks, half blocks, and/or corner blocks in each row *(Quilt Assembly Diagram)*. Check position of blocks carefully; then join blocks in each row. Make 1 of Row 1, 4 of Row 2, 3 of Row 3, and 1 of Row 4.

2. Lay out rows again, checking position to be sure overall design is correct. When satisfied with placement, join rows in order as shown.

(continued)

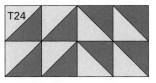

Half Block 4—Make 8.

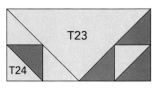

Half Block 5—Make 6.

Half Block 6—Make 4.

Half Block 7—Make 6.

Corner Block 8—Make 2.

Corner Block 9—Make 2.

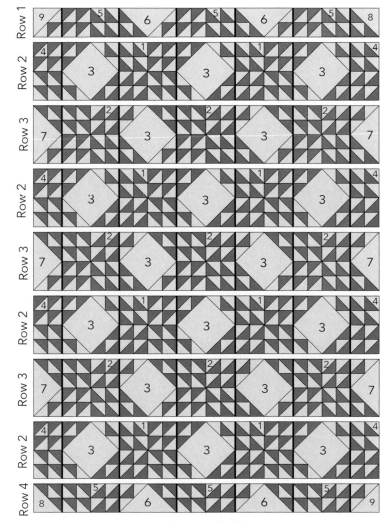

Quilt Assembly Diagram

Adding Borders

Because the inner border is a spacer between the blocks and the pieced border, it is prudent to piece the sawtooth border before adding inner border in order to make any adjustments that might be necessary. See page 20 for more information about spacers.

1. Use remaining triangle-squares to assemble sawtooth border. For each side border, join 34 triangle-squares in a vertical row, sewing light triangles to dark triangles except in middle of row where triangle positions reverse (see photo). For top and bottom borders, make 2 horizontal rows of 28 units each.

2. Measure quilt from top to bottom, omitting seam allowances (approximately 64"); then measure length of pieced side border (approximately 68"). Subtract to determine width of spacer border (68" - 64" = 4")—*finished* border width is half (4" ÷ 2 = 2"), *plus* seam allowances (2½"). Trim Fabric B border strips to appropriate width according to your own measurements. Repeat for top and bottom borders. If width of top and bottom borders differs slightly from side borders, it probably won't be noticeable.

3. When Fabric B border strips are trimmed to correct width, follow instructions on page 20 to trim borders to match length of quilt. Join borders to quilt sides.

4. Measure quilt from side to side; then trim remaining borders to match. Join borders to top and bottom edges of quilt. Press seam allowances toward borders.

5. Join pieced side borders to quilt sides, easing to fit as necessary. Then join top and bottom borders to quilt.

6. Join strips of Fabric C end-to-end in pairs to make 4 accent border strips. Following instructions on page 20, measure quilt from top to bottom; then trim 2 border strips to match length. Join these borders to quilt sides. Measure quilt from side to side; then trim

remaining strips to match. Join borders to top and bottom edges of quilt. Press seam allowances toward accent border.

7. Join outer borders to quilt top in same manner.

Finishing

1. Mark quilting design on top as desired. Quilt shown has diagonal lines of quilting through triangle-squares and a heart motif in large squares. Sawtooth and accent borders are outline-quilted, while inner border has zigzag quilting and outer border has parallel diagonal lines of quilting. Two other quilting suggestions are shown here *(Alternate Quilting Diagrams)*.

2. Divide backing into 2 (2-yard) lengths. Join lengths to assemble backing. Layer backing, batting, and quilt top. (Backing seam parallels top and bottom edges of quilt.) Baste. Quilt as marked or as desired.

3. Cut 8½ yards of 1½"-wide bias binding. See page 26 for instructions on making and applying binding.

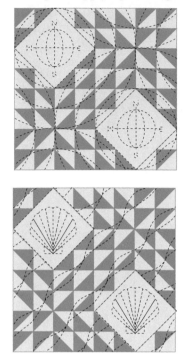

Alternate Quilting Diagrams

Size Variations

	Full/Queen	King
Finished Size	83" x 91"	99" x 99"
Number of Blocks		
Block 1	12	20
Block 2	16	20
Block 3	28	41
Block 4	8	10
Block 5	8	10
Block 6	6	8
Block 7	8	8
Block 8	2	2
Block 9	2	2
Number of Triangle-Squares (includes border)	868	1,172

Materials for Size Variations

		Full/Queen	King
	Fabric A	4½ yards	6 yards
	Fabric B	5⅞ yards	7¼ yards
	Fabric C*	½ yard	½ yard
	Fabric D	2½ yards	3 yards
	Backing fabric	5½ yards	9 yards

* Cut crosswise.

Ocean Waves by Marsha McCloskey, Seattle, Washington, 1994.

Northwind

This variation is similar to Ocean Waves but is easier to piece. Here, one simple block

repeats, rotating to create the look of a complex quilt design.

Northwind by Marsha McCloskey, Seattle, Washington, 1994.

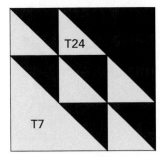

Northwind Block

Materials

■	Fabric A (assorted brick red prints)	1¾ yards total
□	Fabric B (assorted light prints)	1½ yards total
	Fabric C (brown print)	½ yard
	Fabric D (dark brown print)	1⅝ yards
	Binding fabric	⅝ yard
	Backing fabric	3 yards
	Precut batting	72" x 90"

* This quilt is a crib or lap size. Requirements for other sizes are listed on page 104.

Cutting

Instructions are for rotary cutting. To check cutting accuracy, compare rotary-cut pieces to patterns S20, T7, and T24 (see pattern index, page 146). For traditional piecing, use these patterns to make templates.

From Fabric A (red prints), cut:
• 4 (1¾" x 52") lengthwise strips for middle border.
• 9 (10") squares for bias-strip piecing.
• 24 (4⅞") squares. Cut each square in half diagonally to get 48 half-square triangles (T7), 1 for each block. For easy matching, trim points at 4½" (see page 13).
• 48 (2⅞") squares. Cut each square in half diagonally to get 96 half-square triangles (T24), 2 for each block. Trim points at 2½".

From Fabric B (light prints), cut:
• 9 (10") squares for bias-strip piecing.
• 24 (4⅞") squares. Cut each square in half diagonally to get 48 half-square triangles (T7), 1 for each block. Trim points at 4½".
• 48 (2⅞") squares. Cut each square in half diagonally to get 96 half-square triangles (T24), 2 for each block. Trim points at 2½".

From Fabric C (brown print), cut:
• 4 (1¾" x 50") lengthwise strips for inner border.

From Fabric D (dark brown print), cut:
• 4 (4½" x 54") lengthwise strips for outer border.

Bias-Strip Piecing Triangle-Squares

See page 16 for detailed instructions on bias-strip piecing two-triangle squares.

1. With right sides facing, match 1 (10") square of Fabric A with a 10" square of Fabric B.
2. Cutting through both layers, cut squares diagonally from corner to corner to establish true bias (45° angle). Measuring from cut edges, cut 4 sets of 2½"-wide bias strips and 2 sets of leftover corner triangles *(Diagram A)*.
3. Join each pair of bias strips; then join pairs to complete a bias-strip setup as shown *(Diagram B)*. Join corner triangles. Press seam allowances toward darker fabric.
4. Using a square ruler with bias marking, rotary-cut 16 (2½") squares from this setup.
5. Repeat with remaining A and B squares to make a total of 144 two-triangle squares, 3 for each block.

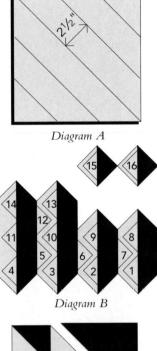

Diagram A

Diagram B

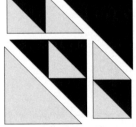

Block Assembly Diagram

Making Blocks

1. For each block, select 3 triangle-squares. From each of fabrics A and B, select 2 T24 triangles and 1 T7 triangle.
2. Sew T24 triangles of Fabric A to both light sides of 1 triangle-square *(Block Assembly Diagram)*. Press seam allowances toward Fabric A triangles.

(continued)

3. Join Fabric B triangles to dark side of remaining 2 triangle-squares as shown. Press seam allowances toward Fabric B triangles. Then join these units to first unit as shown.

4. Join T7 triangles to center unit to complete block. Repeat to make a total of 48 blocks.

Quilt Assembly

1. Lay out blocks in 8 horizontal rows, with 6 blocks in each row *(Row Assembly Diagram)*. Arrange blocks to achieve a pleasing balance of color and contrast. Rotate blocks as shown to make 4 of Row 1 and 4 of Row 2, alternating rows (see photo).

2. Join blocks in rows. Then join rows.

Adding Borders

1. Referring to instructions on page 20, measure quilt from top to bottom; then trim 2 Fabric C border strips to match length. Join borders to quilt sides. Press seam allowances toward borders.

2. Measure quilt from side to side; then trim remaining Fabric C strips to match. Join borders to top and bottom edges of quilt. Press seam allowances toward borders.

3. Join Fabric A border strips to quilt in same manner; then repeat to join Fabric D border strips.

Finishing

1. Mark quilting design on quilt top as desired. Quilt shown has diagonal lines quilted through small triangles and parallel diagonal lines in outer border. Remaining triangles and borders are outline-quilted. Two other quilting suggestions are shown here *(Alternate Quilting Diagrams)*.

2. Divide backing into 2 (1½-yard) lengths. Join lengths to assemble backing. Layer backing, batting, and quilt top. (Backing seam will parallel top and bottom edges). Baste. Quilt as marked or as desired.

Row 1

Row 2

Row Assembly Diagram

Size Variations

	Twin	Full/Queen	King
Finished Size	67½" x 85½"	85½" x 97½"	97½" x 97½"
Number of Blocks	108	168	196
Blocks Set	9 x 12	12 x 14	14 x 14
Number of Triangle-Squares	324	504	588

Materials for Size Variations

		Twin	Full/Queen	King
■	Fabric A	3⅝ yards	5⅛ yards	6⅛ yards
☐	Fabric B	3½ yards	5 yards	6 yards
	Fabric C*	½ yard	½ yard	½ yard
	Fabric D	2¼ yards	2⅝ yards	2⅞ yards
	Binding fabric	¾ yard	¾ yard	¾ yard
	Backing fabric	4¼ yards	5⅞ yards	8⅞ yards

* Cut strips crosswise.

Alternate Quilting Diagrams

3. Cut 6½ yards of 1½"-wide bias binding. See page 26 for instructions on making and applying binding.

Old Maid's Schoolhouse

Alternating two blocks is one of my favorite and most reliable design strategies. This quilt combines a Schoolhouse block that I designed with Old Maid's Puzzle. Terri Shinn's fabric and color choices give this traditional-style quilt a contemporary look. Quick-piecing methods make fast work of the two-triangle squares in the Old Maid's Puzzle blocks.

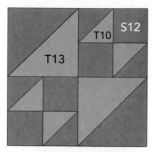

Old Maid's Puzzle Block

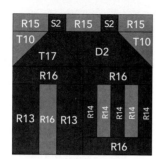

Schoolhouse Block

Materials

■	Fabric A (assorted rust and red prints)	2 yards total
■	Fabric B (assorted gray prints)	3½ yards total
■	Fabric C (assorted yellow prints)	1½ yards total
	Fabric D (gray/brown print for border)	2½ yards
	Binding fabric	¾ yard
	Backing fabric	5½ yards
	Precut batting	81" x 96"

* This quilt fits a twin bed. Requirements for other sizes are listed on page 107.

Cutting

Instructions are for rotary cutting. To check cutting accuracy, compare rotary-cut pieces to patterns S2, S12, R13, R14, R15, R16, D2, T10, T13, and T17 (see pattern index, page 146). For traditional piecing, use these patterns to make templates.

From Fabric A (red prints), cut:
• 4 (3"-wide) crosswise strips. From these, cut 24 rhomboids (D2), 1 for each Schoolhouse block. See page 12 for tips on cutting rhomboids. If you prefer, use more (shorter) strips for a scrappier look.
• 6 (6¼") squares. Cut each square in quarters diagonally to get 24 quarter-square triangles (T17), 1 for each Schoolhouse block.
• 48 (2⅜" x 5½") rectangles (R13), 2 for each Schoolhouse block.
• 72 (1¾" x 5½") rectangles (R16), 3 for each Schoolhouse block.
• 48 (1¾") squares (S2), 2 for each Schoolhouse block.
• 72 (1½" x 4¼") rectangles (R14), 3 for each Schoolhouse block.

From Fabric B (gray prints), cut:
• 6 (13½") squares and 12 (8") squares for bias-strip piecing triangles in Old Maid's Puzzle blocks.
• 96 (3") squares (S12), 4 for each Old Maid's Puzzle block.
• 72 (1¾" x 3") rectangles (R15), 3 for each Schoolhouse block.
• 48 (1½" x 4¼") rectangles (R14), 2 for each Schoolhouse block.
• 24 (1¾" x 5½") rectangles (R16), 1 for each Schoolhouse block.
• 24 (3⅜") squares. Cut each square in half diagonally to get 48 triangles (T10), 2 for each Schoolhouse block.

From Fabric C (yellow prints), cut:
• 6 (13½") squares and 12 (8") squares for bias-strip piecing triangles in Old Maid's Puzzle blocks.

From Fabric D (gray/brown print), cut:
• 4 (6" x 90") lengthwise strips for outer border.

Making Old Maid's Puzzle Blocks

See page 16 for detailed instructions on bias-strip piecing two-triangle squares.
1. First work with 13½" squares of fabrics B and C to make large triangle-squares. With right sides facing, match 1 square of Fabric B with 1 Fabric C square.
2. Cutting through both layers, cut squares diagonally from corner to corner to establish true bias (45° angle). Measuring from cut edges, cut 2 sets of 4½"-wide strips and 2 sets of leftover corner triangles *(Diagram A)*.
3. Join each pair of bias strips; then join pairs to complete a bias-strip setup as shown *(Diagram B)*. Join corner triangles. Press seam allowances toward darker fabric.
4. Using a square ruler with bias marking, rotary-cut 7 (5½") squares from this setup, 2 from corners and 5 from strips *(Diagram B)*.

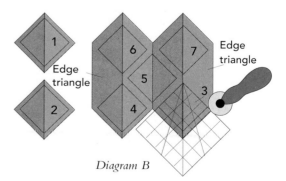

Diagram A

Diagram B

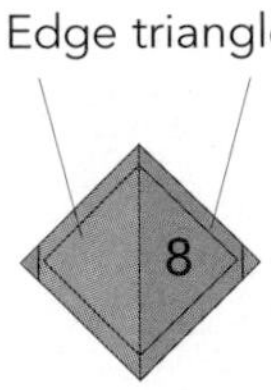

5. To get an eighth triangle-square out of this setup, join remaining edge triangles *(Diagram C)* and cut 1 more square.

6. Repeat with remaining sets of B and C squares to make a total of 48 large 5½" triangle-squares.

7. Use 8" squares of fabrics B and C to make smaller triangle-squares. With right sides facing, cut 1 set of squares to get 2 sets of 3"-wide bias strips and 2 sets of corner triangles *(Diagram D)*. Follow steps above to assemble bias-strip setup and cut 8 triangle-squares. Repeat with remaining 8" B and C squares to make a total of 96 small 3" triangle-squares.

8. For each block, select 2 small triangle-squares, 2 large triangle-squares, and 4 S12 squares of Fabric B.

9. Join 1 S12 to Fabric C side of each small triangle-square *(Old Maid's Puzzle Block Assembly Diagram)*. Press seam allowances toward S12. Join these units in pairs to make 2 four-patch quarter-block units as shown.

10. Join each four-patch to 1 large triangle-square as shown. Press seam allowances toward large triangle-square. Join halves to complete block.

11. Repeat to make a total of 24 Old Maid's Puzzle blocks.

Making Schoolhouse Blocks

1. For each block, select 2 S2, 1 T17, 1 D2, 2 R13, 3 R14, and 3 R16 from Fabric A; then select 2 T10, 2 R14, 3 R15, and 1 R16 from Fabric B. Block is made in 4 sections *(Schoolhouse Block Assembly Diagram)*. Identify pieces for each section.

2. For chimney section, join 2 S2 and 3 R15 in a row as shown.

3. For roof section, join 1 T10 to 1 side of T17. Join second T10 to 1 side of D2. Join T17 and D2 to complete section.

4. For door section, join 1 R13 to each side of Fabric B R16. Join 1 Fabric A

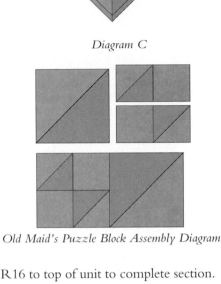

Diagram C

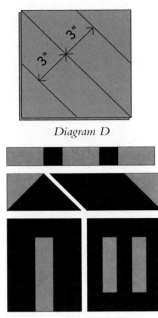

Diagram D

Old Maid's Puzzle Block Assembly Diagram

Schoolhouse Block Assembly Diagram

R16 to top of unit to complete section.

5. For window section, join R14 pieces in a row, alternating fabrics A and B as shown. Sew Fabric A R16 pieces to top and bottom of unit to complete section.

6. Join door and window sections. Add roof and chimney sections to complete block.

7. Repeat to make a total of 24 Schoolhouse blocks.   *(continued)*

Size Variations

	Full	Queen	King
Finished Size	81" x 91"	91" x 91"	101" x 101"
Number of Blocks			
Old Maid's Puzzle	28	32	40
Schoolhouse	28	32	41
Blocks Set	7 x 8	8 x 8	9 x 9
Number of Large Triangle-squares	56	64	80
Number of Small Triangle-squares	112	128	160

Materials for Size Variations

		Full	Queen	King
■	Fabric A	2¾ yards	3 yards	4 yards
▦	Fabric B	3¾ yards	4⅛ yards	5 yards
▧	Fabric C	2 yards	2 yards	2½ yards
	Fabric D	2½ yards	2¾ yards	3 yards
	Binding fabric	¾ yard	¾ yard	¾ yard
	Backing fabric	5½ yards	8¼ yards	9¼ yards

Quilt Assembly

1. Lay out blocks in 8 horizontal rows. Each row alternates 3 Puzzle blocks and 3 Schoolhouse blocks. Row 1 begins with a Schoolhouse block and Row 2 begins with a Puzzle block *(Row Assembly Diagram)*. Lay out 4 of each row, alternating row types. Arrange blocks to achieve a pleasing balance of color and contrast.

2. Join blocks in each row. Then join rows.

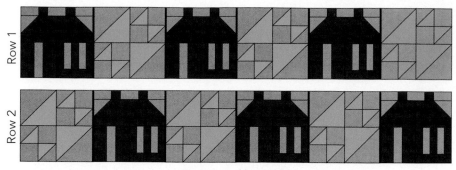

Row Assembly Diagram

Old Maid's Schoolhouse by Terri Shinn, Snohomish, Washington, 1995.
Quilt design by Marsha McCloskey.

Adding Border

1. Referring to instructions on page 20, measure quilt from top to bottom; then trim 2 border strips to match length. Join borders to quilt sides. Press seam allowances toward borders.
2. Measure quilt from side to side; then trim remaining borders to match quilt width. Join borders first to top and bottom edges of quilt. Press seam allowances toward borders.

Finishing

1. Mark quilting design on quilt top as desired. On quilt shown, quilting is a simple grid of vertical and horizontal lines. Two other quilting suggestions are shown here (*Alternate Quilting Diagrams*).
2. Divide backing into 2 (2¾-yard) lengths. Join lengths to assemble backing. Layer backing, batting, and quilt top. Baste. Quilt as marked or as desired.
3. Cut 9½ yards of 1½"-wide bias binding. See page 26 for instructions on making and applying binding.

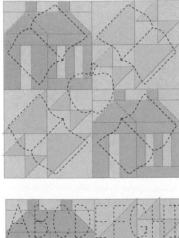

Alternate Quilting Diagrams

Inches, Yards, and Meters

If you are accustomed to the metric system, this chart will be helpful in establishing conversions for some common measurements. Or, if you are buying fabric in the U.S.A., use the decimals column and your calculator to figure cost. For example, if you're buying 1¾ yards of $7.60-a-yard fabric, multiply $7.60 by 1.75 to get a cost of $13.30.

Inches	Fractions	Decimals	Meters
⅛"		.125"	.318cm
¼"		.25"	.635cm
⅜"		.375"	.953cm
½"		.5"	1.27cm
¾"		.75"	1.9cm
1"		1.0"	2.54cm
4½"	⅛ yard	.125 yard	11.43cm
9"	¼ yard	.25 yard	22.86cm
12"	⅓ yard	.333 yard	.3m
13½"	⅜ yard	.375 yard	.3375m
18"	½ yard	.5 yard	.45m
22½"	⅝ yard	.625 yard	.563m
27"	¾ yard	.75 yard	.675m
31½"	⅞ yard	.875 yard	.788m
36"	1 yard	1 yard	.9m
39⅜"	1¹⁄₁₀ yards	1.1 yards	1m
54"	1½ yards	1.5 yards	1.35m
63"	1¾ yards	1.75 yards	1.6m

When you know:	Multiply by:	To find:
inches	2.54	centimeters (cm)
yards	.9	meters (m)

Ohio Star

A large-scale floral print adds visual interest to this simple pieced quilt, made with only three fabrics.

The star blocks are set on point in a zigzag set, joined with large triangles in vertical rows.

This quilt is fast and easy to make because the star points are quick-pieced. Read on for more about this

fun way to take bias-strip piecing one step further to make four-triangle squares.

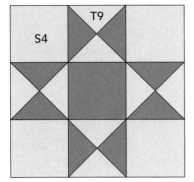

Ohio Star Block

Materials

	Fabric A (navy print, includes binding)	3 yards
	Fabric B (light cream print)	2½ yards
	Fabric C (brown cabbage rose print)	5½ yards
	Backing fabric	6 yards
	Precut batting	90" x 108"

* This quilt fits a full-size bed. In photo at left, quilt is turned sideways to fit a king-size bed. Requirements for other sizes are listed on page 113.

Cutting

Instructions are for rotary cutting. To check cutting accuracy, compare rotary-cut pieces to patterns S4, T6, T9, and T15 (see pattern index, page 146). For traditional piecing, use these patterns to make templates.

From Fabric A (navy print), cut:
• 9 (13½") squares for bias-strip piecing.
• 12 (7⅝") squares. Cut each square in quarters diagonally to get 46 quarter-square triangles (T15) for pieced border (and 2 extra).
• 30 (3½") squares (S4), 1 for each block.
• 1 (¾-yard) piece for binding.

From Fabric B (cream print), cut:
• 9 (13½") squares for bias-strip piecing.
• 120 (3½") squares (S4), 4 for each block.

From Fabric C (brown print), cut:
• 4 (6" x 104") lengthwise strips for outer borders.
• 11 (7⅝") squares. Cut each square in quarters diagonally to get 42 quarter-square triangles (T15) for pieced border (and 2 extra).
• 7 (7¼") squares. Cut each square in half diagonally to get 14 half-square triangles for border corners (T6).

• 3 (13⅝") squares. Cut each square in half diagonally to get 5 half-square triangles for Set Triangle X (and 1 extra).
• 14 (13⅞") squares. Cut each square in quarters diagonally to get 55 quarter-square triangles for Set Triangle Y (and 1 extra).

Bias-Strip Piecing Four-Triangle Squares

See page 16 for detailed instructions on bias-strip piecing two-triangle squares. This technique adds a couple of easy steps to turn those units into four-triangle squares.

1. With right sides facing, match 1 (13½") square of Fabric A with a 13½" square of Fabric B.

2. Cutting through both layers, cut squares in half diagonally to establish true bias (a 45° angle). Measuring from cut edges, cut 4 sets of 3½"-wide bias strips and 2 sets of leftover corner triangles *(Diagram A)*.
3. Join each pair of bias strips; then join pairs to complete a bias-strip setup as shown *(Diagram B)*. Press seam allowances toward dark fabric.
4. Using a square ruler with bias marking, rotary-cut 14 (3⅞") two-triangle squares from this setup.
5. Repeat with remaining sets of A and B squares to make a total of 120 two-triangle squares. (*Note:* Save leftover triangles and bias strips for scrap projects.) *(continued)*

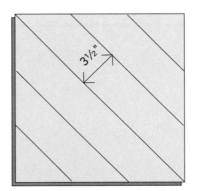

Diagram A

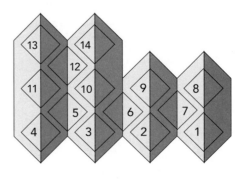

Diagram B

6. With right sides and contrasting fabrics facing, match 2 triangle-squares, nesting opposing seam allowances. Cut both squares in half diagonally *(Photo 1)*. Join each pair of triangles, making 2 four-triangle squares *(Photo 2)*.

7. Repeat to make a total of 120 four-triangle squares for star points.

Making Blocks

1. For each star block, select 4 four-triangle squares, 1 S4 square of Fabric A, and 4 S4 squares of Fabric B. Each unit should be 3½" square.

2. Lay out squares and triangle-squares in 3 horizontal rows with 3 units in each row as shown *(Block Assembly Diagram)*. Join units in each row. Press seam allowances away from triangle-squares.

3. Join rows to complete block. Repeat to make a total of 30 blocks.

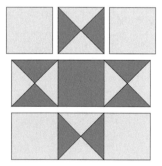

Block Assembly Diagram

Quilt Assembly

1. Lay out blocks on point in 5 vertical rows, with 6 blocks in each row. Fill in rows with set triangles X, Y, and T6 as shown *(Quilt Assembly Diagram)*.

2. In each row, join blocks and set triangles in diagonal units; then join those units to complete each row as shown. Make 1 of Row 1, 2 of Row 2, and 2 of Row 3.

3. Join rows in sequence as shown.

Quilt Assembly Diagram

Adding Borders

1. Use T15 triangles of fabrics A and B for "dogtooth" border. For each side border, join 13 Fabric A triangles and 12 Fabric C triangles in a row, alternating colors as shown. For top and bottom borders, join 10 Fabric A triangles and 9 Fabric C triangles in a row. Press seam allowances toward dark fabric.

2. Join borders to edges of quilt, easing to fit as necessary.

3. To complete border, join 1 T6 to each corner as shown.

4. Referring to instructions on page 20, measure quilt from top to bottom; then trim 2 Fabric C border strips to match length. Join borders to quilt sides. Press seam allowances toward borders.

5. Measure quilt from side to side; then trim remaining borders to match quilt width. Join borders to top and bottom edges. Press seam allowances toward borders.

Finishing

1. Mark quilting design on quilt top as desired. Quilt shown is outline-quilted. Two other quilting suggestions are shown here (*Alternate Quilting Diagrams*).

2. Divide backing into 2 (3-yard) lengths. Join lengths to assemble backing. Layer backing, batting, and quilt top. Baste. Quilt as marked or as desired.

3. Cut 10¼ yards of 1½"-wide bias binding. See page 26 for instructions on making and applying binding.

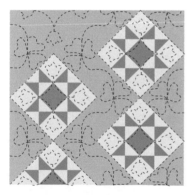

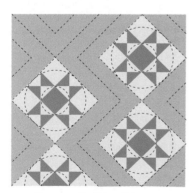

Alternate Quilting Diagrams

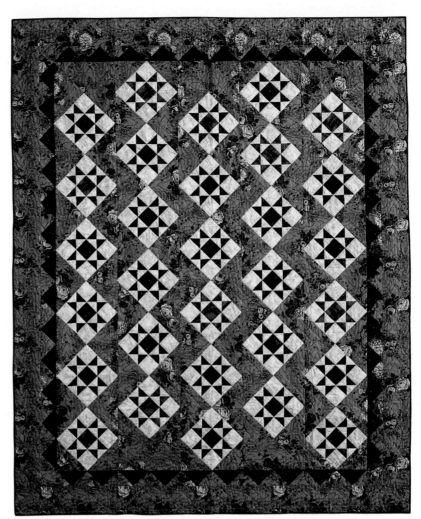

Ohio Star by Marsha McCloskey, Seattle, Washington, 1995. Machine-quilted by Barbara Ford.

Size Variations

	Twin	King
Finished Size	69" x 87½"	94" x 100"
Number of Blocks	20	36
Blocks Set	4 x 5	6 x 6
Number of		
Set Triangle X	4	6
Set Triangle Y	36	66
Set Triangle Z	12	16
T15, Fabric A	38	50
T15, Fabric C	34	

Materials for Size Variations

	Fabric A	2¼ yards	3 yards
	Fabric B	1⅝ yards	2⅞ yards
	Fabric C	3¾ yards	5⅝ yards
	Backing fabric	5⅜ yards	8⅝ yards

Storm at Sea

The waves and circles in *Storm at Sea* are illusions created by the varying angles of the star-spangled patchwork. Inspired by a quilt in *Quilts Japan* magazine, Annette Anderson changed the piecing and coloring, choosing a wide variety of light and dark scraps to make this lively quilt.

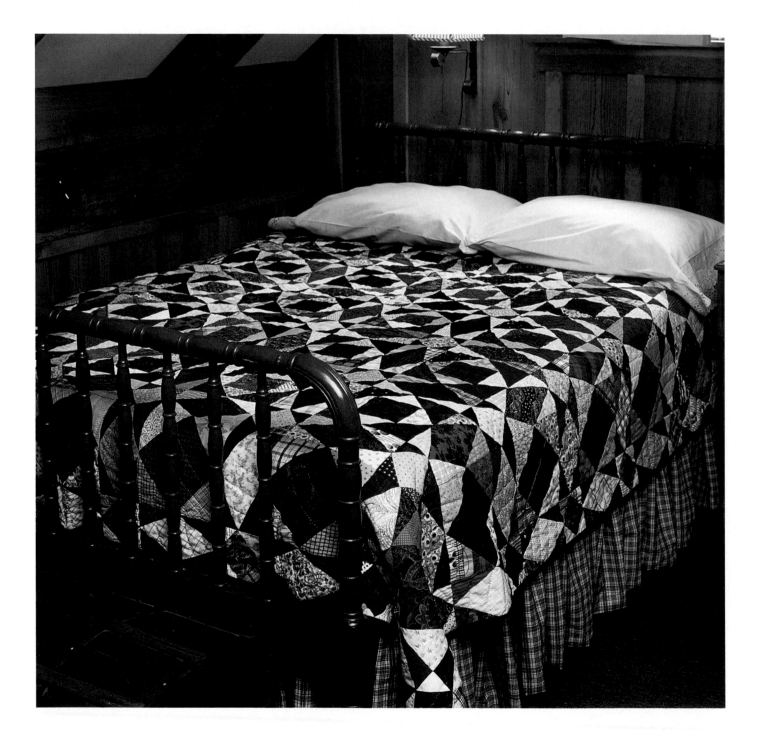

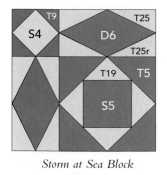

Storm at Sea Block

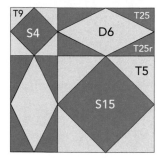

Storm at Sea Border Block

Cutting

Instructions are for rotary cutting. To check cutting accuracy, compare rotary-cut pieces to patterns D6, S4, S5, S15, T5, T9, T19, and T25 (see pattern index, page 146). For traditional piecing, use these patterns to make templates.

Pattern D6 is not a 45° diamond, so the dimensions don't line up with lines on a cutting ruler. To cut diamonds, make a paper template of the pattern and tape the template under your ruler. Align the bottom edge of the template with the edge of the ruler so the template can be a guide to cut diamonds from strips *(Diagram A)*. See page 13 for more information on cutting rhomboids from strips.

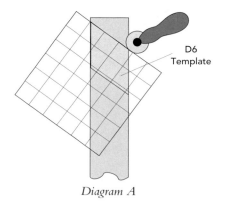

Diagram A

Approximate finished size: 94" x 94"* • Blocks: 49 (12¾") blocks

Materials

	Fabric A (assorted dark prints)	5½ yards total
	Fabric B (assorted light prints)	5 yards
	Binding	¾ yard
	Backing fabric	8¼ yards
	Precut batting	120" x 120"

* This quilt fits a queen-size bed. Requirements for other sizes are listed on page 118.

From Fabric A (dark prints), cut:
• 20 (4⅜" x 22") strips. From these, cut 60 D6 diamonds.
• 24 (6½") squares (S15).
• 50 (5⅛") squares. Cut each square in half diagonally to get 100 half-square triangles (T5). For easy matching, trim points to 4¾" (see page 13).
• 25 (4¾") squares (S5).
• 28 (3½") squares (S4).
• 72 (3") squares. Cut each square in half diagonally to get 144 half-square triangles (T9). Trim points to 2⅝".
• 104 (2¹³⁄₁₆" x 5⁹⁄₁₆") rectangles. With right sides facing, match rectangles in pairs. Cut each rectangle pair in half diagonally *(Diagram B)* to get 104 triangles (T25) and 104 triangles reversed (T25r). Trim points as shown on pattern.

From Fabric B (light prints), cut:
• 18 (4⅜" x 22") strips. From these, cut 52 D6 diamonds.
• 48 (5⅛") squares. Cut each square in half diagonally to get 96 half-square triangles (T5). Trim points to 4¾".

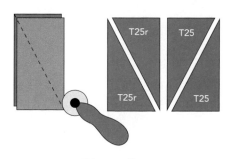

Diagram B

• 50 (3⅞") squares. Cut each square in half diagonally to get 100 half-square triangles (T19). Trim points to 3½".
• 36 (3½") squares (S4).
• 56 (3") squares. Cut each square in half diagonally to get 112 half-square triangles (T9). Trim points to 2⅝".
• 120 (2¹³⁄₁₆" x 5⁹⁄₁₆") rectangles. Cut pairs of rectangles in half diagonally *(Diagram B)* to get 120 triangles (T25) and 120 triangles reversed (T25r). Trim points as shown on pattern.

Making Blocks

You might not notice at a glance, but there are 2 blocks in this quilt. There are 25 Storm at Sea blocks in the center of the quilt and 24 border blocks around the outside edge (see photo on page 118). The Storm at Sea block is made in 3 units. Three similar units make up the border block—units 4 and 5 reverse placement of light and dark fabrics, while Unit 6 has a larger center square.

To make this quilt scrappy, don't plan ahead. Make the units before you assemble any blocks, concentrating on placement of light and dark fabrics. Then join units to make blocks (and extra border units), letting fabrics come together randomly. *(continued)*

1. For each Unit 1, select 1 S4 square of Fabric B and 4 different T9 triangles of Fabric A *(Unit 1 Diagram)*. Join triangles to sides of square. Make 36 of Unit 1, 25 for blocks, 10 for border units, and 1 extra for border row.

2. For each Unit 2, select 2 T25 triangles and 2 T25r triangles of Fabric B, as well as 1 D6 diamond of Fabric A *(Unit 2 Diagram)*. Join triangles to sides of diamond. Make 60 of Unit 2, 50 for blocks and 10 for border units.

3. For each Unit 3, select 4 T5 triangles and 1 S5 square of Fabric A, as well as 4 T19 triangles of Fabric B *(Unit 3 Diagram)*. Join T19 triangles to sides of S5 square; then join T5 triangles as shown. Make 25 of Unit 3 for blocks.

4. For each Unit 4, select 1 S4 square of Fabric A and 4 different T9 triangles of Fabric B *(Unit 4 Diagram)*. Join triangles to sides of square. Make 28 of Unit 4, 24 for border blocks and 4 for border units.

5. For each Unit 5, select 2 T25 triangles and 2 T25r triangles of Fabric A, as well as 1 D6 diamond of Fabric B *(Unit 5 Diagram)*. Join triangles to sides of diamond. Make 52 of Unit 5, 48 for border blocks and 4 for border units.

6. For each Unit 6, select 4 T5 triangles of Fabric B and 1 S15 square of Fabric A *(Unit 6 Diagram)*. Join triangles to sides of square. Make 24 of Unit 6 for border blocks.

7. For each block, select 1 of Unit 1, 2 of Unit 2, and 1 of Unit 3 *(Block Assembly Diagram)*. Join Unit 1 to 1 end of a Unit 2; then join remaining Unit 2 to 1 side of Unit 3. Join units to complete block. Repeat to make a total of 25 blocks.

8. For each border block, select 1 of Unit 4, 2 of Unit 5, and 1 of Unit 6 *(Border Block Assembly Diagram)*. Join units in same manner as before. Make a total of 24 border blocks.

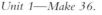

Unit 1—Make 36.

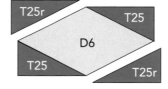

Unit 2—Make 60.

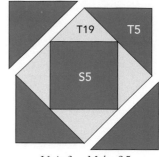

Unit 3—Make 25.

Unit 4—Make 28.

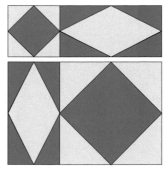

Unit 5—Make 52.

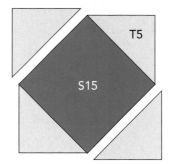

Unit 6—Make 24.

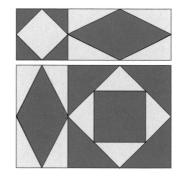

Block Assembly Diagram

Border Block Assembly Diagram

9. Join each remaining Unit 2 to a Unit 1 to make 10 of border Unit 7 *(Unit 7 Diagram)*. You should have 1 Unit 1 left over.

10. Join each remaining Unit 4 to a Unit 5 to make 4 of border Unit 8 *(Unit 8 Diagram)*.

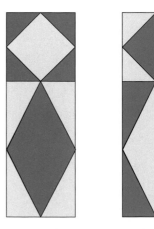

Unit 7—Make 10.   Unit 8—Make 4.

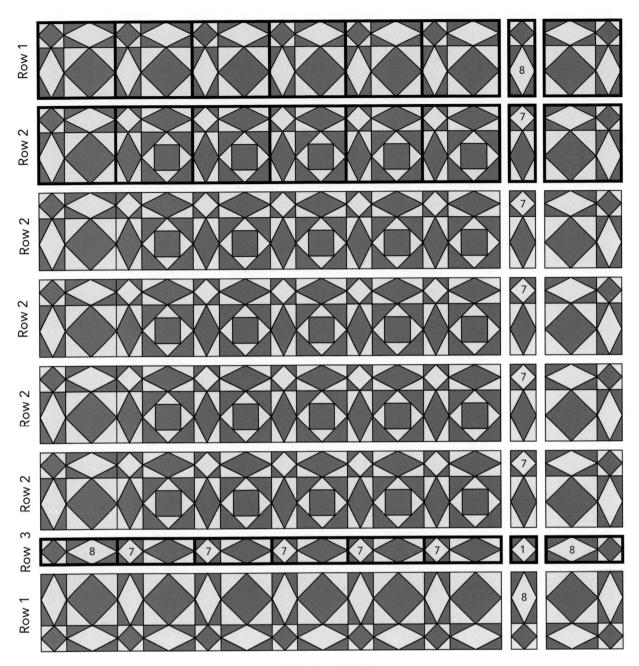

Quilt Assembly Diagram

Quilt Assembly

The magic of this quilt is how well the blocks blend once joined—the blocks disappear into what seems to be an overall design. Refer to *Quilt Assembly Diagram* closely to place blocks and border units correctly in each row.

1. For each Row 1, select 7 border blocks and 1 of Unit 8. Lay out 1 of Row 1 for first row of quilt and another of Row 1 for bottom row as shown.

2. For each Row 2, select 5 blocks, 2 border blocks, and 1 of Unit 7. Lay out 5 of Row 2 as shown.

3. Use remaining units 1, 7, and 8 to lay out 1 of Row 3 as shown.

4. Arrange blocks to achieve a pleasing balance of color and contrast. When satisfied with placement of blocks, join blocks and border units in each row. Then join rows as shown to complete quilt top. *(continued)*

Finishing

1. Mark quilting design on quilt top as desired. Quilt shown is quilted in the all-over Baptist Fan motif (see pattern, page 23). Two other quilting suggestions are shown here *(Alternate Quilting Diagrams)*.

2. Divide the backing fabric into 3 (2¾-yard) lengths. Cut 1 panel in half lengthwise and discard 1 half. Join remaining panels lengthwise to assemble backing. Layer backing, batting, and quilt top. Baste. Quilt as marked or as desired.

3. Cut 11 yards of 1½"-wide bias binding. See page 26 for instructions on making and applying binding.

Size Variations

	Twin	Full	King
Finished Size	68" x 93½"	81" x 94"	106" x 106"
Number of Blocks	15	20	36
Border Blocks	20	22	28
Border Unit 7	8	9	12
Border Unit 8	4	4	4
Blocks Set	5 x 7	6 x 7	8 x 8

Materials for Size Variations

	Twin	Full	King
Fabric A	4⅛ yards	5⅛ yards	7½ yards
Fabric B	3⅞ yards	4½ yards	6⅛ yards
Binding fabric	⅝ yard	¾ yard	¾ yard
Backing fabric	5¾ yards	5¾ yards	9¾ yards

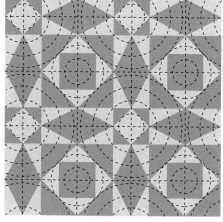

Alternate Quilting Diagrams

Storm at Sea by Annette Anderson, Ferndale, Washington, 1994.

Spools & Bobbins

A block's diagonal is 40% longer than its side, so setting blocks on point often lets you make a nice-sized quilt with fewer blocks. I had fun figuring out how best to make half-blocks and quarter-blocks for the side triangles in this diagonal set. I needed the partial blocks because I chose this diagonal set with lattices to get the most out of 18 blocks.

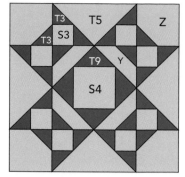

Spools & Bobbins Block

Materials

Fabric A (assorted light blue prints)	4 yards total
Fabric B (assorted dark blue prints)	2 yards total
Fabric C (blue for lattice, border, binding)	2⅝ yards
Fabric D (medium blue plaid)	2⅝ yards
Backing fabric	5¼ yards
Precut batting	90" x 108"

* This quilt fits a full or queen-sized bed. Requirements for other sizes are on page 125.

Cutting

Instructions are for rotary cutting. To check cutting accuracy, compare rotary-cut pieces to patterns S3, S4, S11, T3, T5, T9, and T19 (see pattern index, page 146). Also use patterns X, Y, and Z on page 125. For traditional piecing, use these patterns to make templates.

Following these instructions, cut whole pieces for edges of half-blocks and quarter-blocks—it's easier than cutting a lot of odd shapes individually. Trim these units as you assemble partial blocks.

From Fabric A (light prints), cut:
- 212 (2") squares (S3), 8 for each block, 6 for each half-block, and 2 for each quarter-block.
- 18 (3½") squares (S4), 1 for each block.
- 24 (7¼") squares. Cut each square in quarters diagonally to get 96 quarter-square triangles (T5), 4 for each block, 2 for each half-block, and 1 for each quarter-block.
- 110 (3½") squares. Use Cut-away Triangle X to trim 1 corner from each square to make 110 Z pieces, 4 for each block, 3 for each half-block, and 2 for each quarter-block. See Cutting Corners, opposite, for details on this technique.

- 55 (3⅞") squares. Cut each square in half diagonally to get 110 half-square triangles. Trim points to 3½" (see page 13.) Use Cut-away Triangle X to trim corner from triangles to make 110 Y trapezoids, 4 for each block, 3 for each half-block, and 2 for each quarter-block.
- 2 (3") squares. Cut each square in half diagonally to get 4 triangles (T9), 1 for each quarter-block.
- 3 (5½") squares. Cut each square in quarters diagonally to get 10 (and 2 extra) quarter-square triangles (T19), 1 for each half-block.
- 17 (2⅝") squares (S11) for lattice cornerstones.
- 4 (4¼") squares. Cut each square in quarters diagonally to get 14 (and 2 extra) quarter-square triangles (T9) for ends of lattice rows.

From Fabric B (dark prints), cut:
- 302 (2⅜") squares. Cut each square in half diagonally to get 604 half-square triangles (T3), 24 for each block, 14 for each half-block, and 8 for each quarter-block. Trim points to 2".
- 48 (3") squares. Cut each square in half diagonally to get 96 half-square triangles (T9), 4 for each block, 2 for each half-block, and 1 for each quarter-block. Trim points to 2⅝".

From Fabric C (blue), cut:
- 2 (2⅝" x 92") lengthwise border strips.
- 48 (2⅝" x 12½") lattice strips.
- 1 (24" x 37") piece for binding.

From Fabric D (blue plaid), cut:
- 6 (4½" x 92") lengthwise border strips.

Making Blocks

1. For each block, select 1 S4, 4 T5, 8 S3, 4 Y, and 4 Z from Fabric A. From Fabric B, select 4 T9 and 24 T3. Refer to unit diagrams to sort pieces into units for assembly.

2. For Unit A1, join 2 T9 triangles to opposite sides of S4 square *(Unit A1 Diagram)*. Press seam allowances toward triangles. Join 2 more T9 triangles to remaining sides of square to complete 1 Unit A1.

3. For Unit B, join a T3 triangle to 1 Y piece as shown *(Unit B Diagram)*. Press seam allowance toward triangle. Make 4 of Unit B.

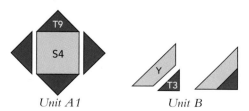

Unit A1   *Unit B*

Cutting Corners with Paper Templates

A cut-away triangle is a paper template sometimes used in rotary cutting to trim corners from triangles to create trapezoids, like the ones in *Spools & Bobbins*. It is also used to trim squares to make octagons like those in some feathered star blocks.

1. Start with a triangle or square, cut with the grain direction as indicated in instructions.

2. Make a paper template of the cut-away triangle given with each project. Tape the template under the cutting ruler, aligning outside edges of pattern and ruler *(photo at right)*.

3. Position ruler as shown, matching corner of template with corner of fabric piece. Trim corners from fabric to make desired shape.

4. For Unit C, join 2 T3 triangles to adjacent sides of an S3 square *(Unit C Diagram)*. Press seam allowances toward triangles. Make 8 of Unit C.
5. For Unit D, join a T3 triangle to trimmed edge of 1 Z piece *(Unit D Diagram)*. Press seam allowance toward triangle. Make 4 of Unit D.
6. For Unit AB, join 2 B units to opposite sides of Unit A as shown

(Unit AB Diagram). Press seam allowances toward B units. Join remaining B units to Unit A to complete Unit AB.
7. For Unit CC, join a Unit C to both short legs of a T5 triangle *(Unit CC Diagram)*. Make 4 of Unit CC.
8. Lay out assembled units in 3 horizontal rows *(Block Assembly Diagram)*. For top row, join 1 Unit D to each side of 1 Unit CC. Press seam allowances

toward D units. For middle row, join 1 Unit CC to each side of Unit AB; then press seam allowances toward AB unit. Make bottom row in same manner as top row. Join rows to complete block.
9. Repeat to make a total of 18 blocks.

(continued)

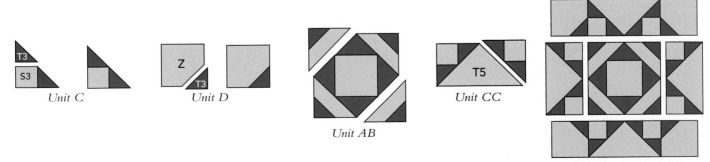

Unit C   *Unit D*   *Unit AB*   *Unit CC*

Block Assembly Diagram

Making Partial Blocks

If you make whole blocks and cut them in half diagonally, the cut edge is left without seam allowances and points are lost when you add borders. Also, the outside edge will be bias, a stretchy situation I'd rather avoid. So I make certain that trimmed pieces include proper seam allowances and I stay-stitch bias edges.

For half-blocks and quarter-blocks, trim units B and D before assembling blocks.

1. For each half-block, select 1 T19, 2 T5, 4 S3, 3 Y, and 3 Z from Fabric A. From Fabric B, select 14 T3 and 2 T9. Use these pieces to make 3 of Unit B, 2 of Unit CC, and 3 of Unit D as for full block. Join T9 triangles to legs of T19 triangle to make 1 of Unit A2 as shown *(Unit A2 Diagram)* and press seam allowances toward T19.

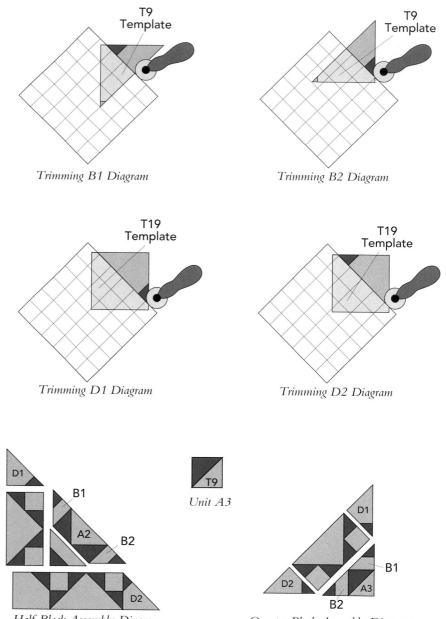

Trimming B1 Diagram

Trimming B2 Diagram

Trimming D1 Diagram

Trimming D2 Diagram

Unit A2

2. Make a paper template of T9, trimming both triangle points as indicated on pattern (page 151). Tape template under cutting ruler, aligning short leg of triangle with ruler edge as shown *(Trimming B1 Diagram)*. Select 1 Unit B to be trimmed. Align long leg of template with outside edge of pieced unit. Trim along edge of ruler, cutting to right of unit corner as shown. Discard excess. Trim second B unit in same manner, realigning ruler and pieced unit as shown *(Trimming B2 Diagram)* to cut a mirror-image unit.

3. Select 2 of Unit D to be trimmed. Make a paper template of T19 as before and tape it under cutting ruler, aligning long leg of triangle with ruler edge as shown *(Trimming D1 Diagram)*. Trim along edge of ruler, cutting to right of unit corners as shown. Discard excess. Trim second D unit in same manner, realigning pieced unit as

Unit A3

Half-Block Assembly Diagram

Quarter-Block Assembly Diagram

shown *(Trimming D2 Diagram)* to cut a mirror-image unit.

4. Lay out assembled units in rows *(Half-Block Assembly Diagram)*. Join rows to complete half-block.

5. Repeat to make a total of 10 half-blocks. Stay-stitch long edge of pieced triangles to prevent bias from stretching.

6. For each quarter-block, select 1 T9, 1 T5, 2 S3, 2 Y, and 2 Z from Fabric A. From Fabric B, select 8 T3 and 1 T9. Use these pieces to make 2 of Unit B, 1

of Unit CC, and 2 of Unit D as for full block. Join T9 triangles to make 1 of Unit A3 as shown *(Unit A3 Diagram)*.

7. Trim units B1, B2, D1, and D2 as described in steps 2 and 3 above. Join assembled units as shown to complete quarter-block *(Quarter-Block Assembly Diagram)*. Make a total of 4 quarter-blocks. Stay-stitch both short legs of pieced triangles to prevent bias from stretching. *(continued)*

Spools & Bobbins by Marsha McCloskey, Seattle, Washington, 1995.
Machine-quilted by Barbara Ford.

Quilt Assembly

To assemble this quilt, set blocks on the diagonal, alternating with lattice strips. Fill in around the edge of the quilt with partial blocks.

1. Lay out blocks in diagonal rows, alternating blocks with lattice strips (*Quilt Assembly Diagram*). Position a half-block at ends of each row and quarter-blocks at quilt corners as shown. Between block rows, lay out rows of lattice and cornerstones (S11), with T9 triangles at ends of lattice rows. Arrange blocks and partial blocks for a pleasing balance of fabrics and contrast.

2. For block rows, join blocks, partial blocks, and lattice strips in diagonal rows. Press seam allowances toward lattice. For lattice rows, join lattice strips, cornerstones, and edge triangles in diagonal rows.

3. Join rows as shown. Quilt should measure approximately 60½" x 80½" before adding borders.

Adding Borders

On this quilt, top and bottom borders are plain, but side borders are pieced in 3 vertical strips.

1. To assemble side borders, join Fabric D strips to both sides of each Fabric C strip. Press seam allowances toward Fabric C.

2. Referring to instructions on page 20, measure quilt from top to bottom; then trim pieced border unit to match length. Join borders to quilt sides. Press seam allowances toward borders.

3. Measure quilt from side to side; then trim remaining Fabric D borders to match quilt width. Join borders to top and bottom edges.

Quilt Assembly Diagram

Finishing

1. Mark quilting design on quilt top as desired. Quilt shown is outline-quilted, with a simple scallop and diamond motif quilted in lattices and borders.

2. Divide backing into 2 (2⅝-yard) lengths. Join lengths to assemble backing. Layer backing, batting, and quilt top. Baste. Quilt as marked or as desired.

3. Cut 10 yards of 1½"-wide bias binding. See page 26 for instructions on making and applying binding.

Size Variations

	Twin	King
Finished Size	61" x 88½"	101" x 108½"
Number of Blocks	11	32
Blocks Set	2 x 4	4 x 5
Number of Half-Blocks	8	14
Number of Quarter-Blocks	4	4
Number of Lattice Strips	32	80
Number of Cornerstones	10	31
Number of Edge Triangles	12	18

Materials for Size Variations

		Twin	King
	Fabric A	2¾ yards	5¾ yards
	Fabric B	1⅛ yards	2¾ yards
	Fabric C	2⅝ yards	3⅛ yards
	Fabric D	2⅝ yards	3 yards
	Backing fabric	5¼ yards	9¼ yards

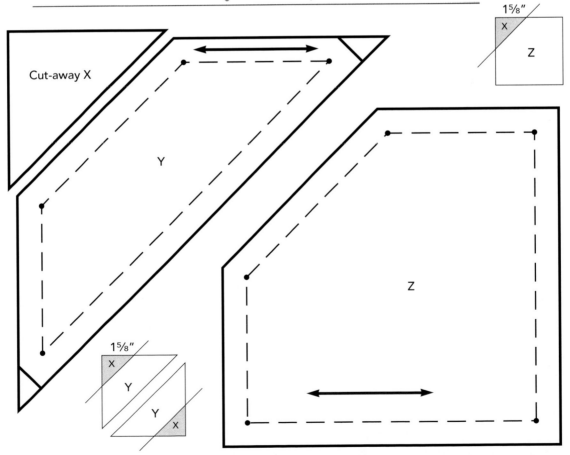

LeMoyne Star

You can bring order to a scrap quilt by using a consistent background fabric. I started

this quilt with muslin and some sample swatches. Some prints appear in different color ways,

a situation I used to avoid as too limited. But in old quilts, I often find the same print in

different colors as if the quiltmaker had swatches that she used like I did.

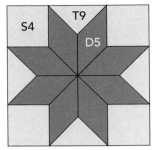

LeMoyne Star Block

Materials

▩	Fabric A (assorted prints)	3½ yards
▨	Fabric B (muslin, including binding)	5½ yards
	Backing fabric	7⅞ yards
	Precut batting	90" x 108"

* This quilt fits a full or queen-sized bed. Requirements for other sizes are listed on page 130.

Cutting

Instructions are for rotary cutting. To check cutting accuracy, compare rotary-cut pieces to patterns D5, S3, S4, R8, and T19 (see pattern index, page 146). For traditional piecing, use these patterns to make templates.

Note: Cut all strips lengthwise.

From Fabric A (assorted prints), cut:
• 8 (2" x 74") strips for pieced borders.
• 26 (2⅝" x 22") strips. From these, cut 128 D5 diamonds, 8 for each block. See page 12 for tips on cutting diamonds from strips.
• 80 (2" x 10¾") strips, 2 for each lattice unit.
• 148 (2") squares (S3) for nine-patches and border corners.

From Fabric B (muslin), cut:
• 4 (3½" x 90") strips for outer borders.
• 4 (2" x 74") strips for pieced borders.
• 4 (5" x 64") strips for inner borders.
• 40 (2" x 10¾") strips, 1 for each lattice unit.
• 1 (20" x 30") piece for binding.
• 16 (5½") squares. Cut each square in quarters diagonally to get 64 quarter-square triangles (T19), 4 for each block.
• 64 (3½") squares (S4), 4 for each block.
• 173 (2") squares (S3) for nine-patches and border corners.
• 8 (2" x 3½") rectangles (R8) for pieced border corners.

Making Blocks

The LeMoyne Star looks like simple patchwork, but the piecing requires set-in seams. Special instructions for sewing set-in seams are on page 129.

1. For each star, select 8 diamonds, 4 triangles, and 4 S4 squares.

2. Following instructions on page 129, make 4 of Unit 1 using diamonds and triangles.

3. To make Unit 2, add a square to right edge of Unit 1. With right sides facing and square on top, begin stitching with a backtack at inner seam line; then sew to raw edge *(Diagram A)*. Make 4 of Unit 2. Press seam allowances toward diamonds.

4. Unit 3 is made with 2 of Unit 2. With right sides facing, match square of 1 Unit 2 to diamond of second unit *(Diagram B)*. With square on top, stitch from outside edge, ending with a backtack at inner seam line.

5. With right sides facing, align unstitched edges of diamonds, folding other pieces out of the way. Pin-match diamonds; then add more pins so you can remove positioning pin. Begin sewing with a backtack at inner seam line *(Diagram C)* and stitch through Unit 1 seams to edge of fabric. Press diamond seams open and corner-square seams toward center of block. Make 2 of Unit 3 *(Diagram D)*.

(continued)

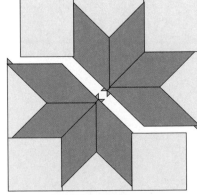

Diagram A

Diagram B

Diagram C

Diagram D

6. To join Unit 3s, sew squares to diamonds as described in Step 4.

7. With right sides facing, use a positioning pin to match diamonds at center. Pin seam securely and remove positioning pin before sewing *(Diagram E)*. Backtack at top seam line and stitch precisely through center, ending with a backtack at seam line. Press seam allowance open. Press corner seam allowances toward diamonds *(Diagram F)*.

8. Repeat to make a total of 16 star blocks.

Making Corner-stones and Lattice

1. For each Nine-Patch, select 4 S3 squares of Fabric A and 5 S3 squares of Fabric B.

2. Join squares in 3 rows of 3 squares each, placing Fabric B at corners and center *(Nine-Patch Assembly Diagram)*. Press seam allowances toward Fabric A squares.

3. Join rows to complete 1 Nine-Patch. Press seam allowances toward center row.

4. Repeat to make a total of 33 Nine-Patches for cornerstones and border corners.

5. For each lattice unit, select 2 (2" x 10¾") strips of Fabric A and 1 same-size strip of Fabric B. Sew Fabric A strips to sides of Fabric B strip as shown *(Lattice Unit Diagram)*. Press seam allowances toward Fabric B strip. Repeat to make a total of 40 lattice units.

Quilt Assembly

1. For Row 1, join 5 Nine-Patches and 4 lattice units *(Quilt Assembly Diagram)*. Make 5 of Row 1.

2. For Row 2, join 5 lattice units and 4 star blocks as shown. Make 4 of Row 2.

3. Join rows as shown.

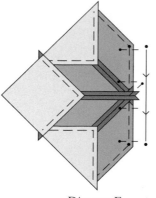

Diagram E

Diagram F

Nine-Patch Assembly Diagram

Lattice Unit—Make 40.

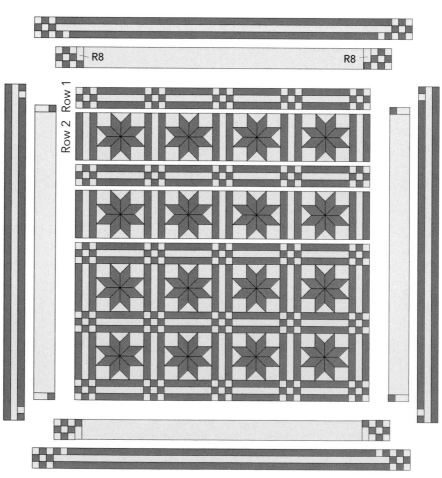

Quilt Assembly Diagram

Adding Borders

1. Join 1 S3 square of Fabric A to each R8 rectangle.

2. Referring to instructions on page 20, measure quilt from top to bottom and side to side. Trim 5"-wide borders to fit; then trim each strip another 3" to allow for R8 units.

3. Join an R8 unit to both ends of each trimmed border strip. Join 2 borders to quilt sides *(Quilt Assembly Diagram)*.

4. Join a Nine-Patch to ends of 2 remaining borders. Add borders to top and bottom edges of quilt.

5. Measure quilt again and trim 4 (2"-wide) Fabric A border strips to fit (approximately 67"). Then trim another 6" from each strip to allow for S3 squares. Join S3 squares of fabrics A and B to each end of strip as shown.

6. Determine length of this pieced border strip. Trim remaining 2"-wide strips of fabrics A and B to match (approximately 73").

7. Join all 2"-wide border strips to make 4 border units as shown. Join 2 of these to quilt sides. Join a Nine-Patch to ends of 2 remaining border units; then sew borders to top and bottom edges of quilt.

8. Measure quilt again and trim 3½"-wide borders to fit. Join 2 strips to quilt sides; then sew 2 remaining borders to top and bottom edges. Press seam allowances towards borders.

(continued)

Sewing Set-in Seams

You'll need to sew set-in seams to make the LeMoyne Star block and Peony block (page 132). When three seams come together in a Y angle, use this technique to set the pieces together.

When sewing a set-in seam, don't stitch across the seam allowance as you do on most patchwork. I use a pencil to lightly mark the seam allowance on the wrong side of the fabric so I won't stitch beyond the ¼" seam line. (In diagrams, this point is indicated by a black dot.)

For example, look at Unit 1 of the LeMoyne Star. This unit consists of two diamonds and one triangle.

1. With right sides facing, match 1 diamond to short leg of 1 triangle *(Diagram A)*. With triangle on top, begin at ¼" seam line and sew 2 stitches forward and 2 stitches back. Take care not to stitch into seam allowance. Stitch to edge of fabric (no need to backtack here because another seam will cross and hold this seam in place). Clip thread and take work out of sewing machine.

2. With right sides facing, match another diamond to second short leg of triangle. With triangle on top, sew from outside edge *(Diagram B)*. End with a backtack at seam line.

3. With right sides facing, match points and edges of diamonds. Fold triangle out of the way. Begin sewing with a backtack at inner seam line and stitch to edge of fabric *(Diagram C)*.

4. Press center seam open and other 2 seams toward diamonds *(Diagram D)*. Trim seam allowances even with unit edges.

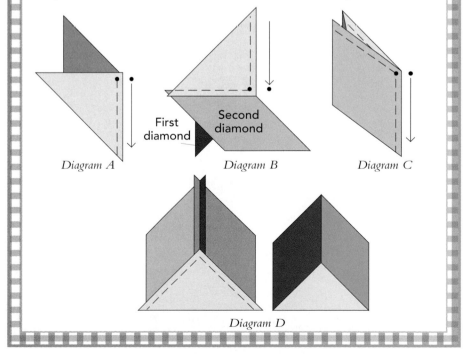

Diagram A   First diamond   Second diamond   *Diagram B*   *Diagram C*

Diagram D

Finishing

1. Mark quilting design on quilt top as desired. Quilt shown is machine-quilted, including scroll and zigzag designs in borders. Muslin borders will show off fancy quilting. Two other quilting suggestions are shown here *(Alternate Quilting Diagrams)*.

2. Divide backing into 3 (2⅝-yard) lengths. Cut 1 piece in half lengthwise; discard 1 half. Join 2 wide panels to sides of remaining narrow panel to make backing. Layer backing, batting, and quilt top. Baste. Quilt as marked or as desired.

3. Cut 10 yards of 1½"-wide bias binding. See page 26 for instructions on making and applying binding.

Size Variations

	Twin	King
Finished Size	58½" x 88"	103" x 103"
Number of Blocks	8	25
Blocks Set	2 x 4	5 x 5
Number of Nine-Patches	23	44
Number of Lattice Units	22	60

Materials for Size Variations

		Twin	King
	Fabric A	2⅝ yards	5¼ yards
	Fabric B	4¼ yards	7⅜ yards
	Backing fabric	5½ yards	9⅝ yards

Alternate Quilting Diagrams

Tying

Pressed for time? Tying is a fast and easy way to secure the quilt layers. It's the best way to work with thick batting for puffy comforters. Tying is also fine for polyester batting, but not for cotton or silk batting, which requires close quilting. Use pearl cotton or sportweight yarn for ties; these are stable enough to stay tightly tied. You'll need a sharp needle with an eye large enough to accommodate the yarn.

Thread the needle with about 7" of thread, but do not knot the end. Starting in the center of your basted quilt top, take a small stitch through all three layers. Clip the thread, leaving a tail about 3" long on each side of the stitch *(Diagram 1)*. Tie the two tails in a tight double knot *(Diagram 2)*. Make a tie at least every 6" across the quilt surface. Trim the tails of all knots to the same length.

Bind the quilt as described on page 26. If your quilt has thick batting, you'll want to cut wider binding strips.

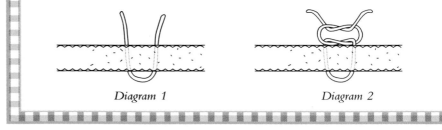

Diagram 1   *Diagram 2*

LeMoyne Star by Marsha McCloskey, Seattle, Washington, 1995.
Machine-quilted by Barbara Ford.

Peony

The Peony block is based on the LeMoyne Star, with two diamonds dropped out
to make room for appliquéd leaves and a stem. A piecing trick called partial seaming
lets you appliqué the stem sides before you sew the seams. Joan Dawson made this quilt
in ever-popular pink and green, but it is also smashing in traditional red, green, and white.

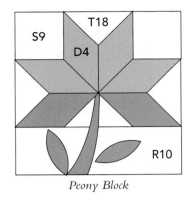

Peony Block

Materials

	Fabric A (assorted pink prints)	1½ yards total
	Fabric B (assorted green prints)	¾ yard total
	Fabric C (white)	3 yards
	Fabric D (mint green print)	4¼ yards
	Binding fabric (pink)	¾ yard
	Backing fabric	7½ yards
	Precut batting	90" x 108"

* This quilt fits a full or queen-sized bed. Requirements for other sizes are listed on page 136.

Cutting

Instructions are for rotary cutting. To check cutting accuracy, compare rotary-cut pieces to patterns D4, S9, R10, T6, T15, and T18 (see pattern index, page 146). Also use appliqué patterns on page 136. For traditional piecing, use these patterns to make templates.

Cut and prepare pieces for appliqué using your preferred appliqué technique. For hand appliqué, add seam allowances when cutting pieces from fabric.

From Fabric A (pink prints), cut:
• 11 (2⅜"-wide) crosswise strips. From these, cut 120 D4 diamonds, 4 for each block. See page 12 for instructions on cutting diamonds from strips.
• 14 (7⅝") squares. Cut each square in quarters diagonally to get 56 quarter-square triangles (T15) for dogtooth border.

From Fabric B (green prints), cut:
• 4 (2⅜"-wide) crosswise strips. From these, cut 60 D4 diamonds, 2 for each block.
• 30 stems, 1 for each block.
• 60 leaves, 2 for each block.

From Fabric C (white), cut:
• 13 (7⅝") squares. Cut each square in quarters diagonally to get 52 quarter-square triangles (T15) for dogtooth border.
• 30 (5") squares. Cut each square in quarters diagonally to get 120 quarter-square triangles (T18), 4 for each block.
• 30 (3⅛" x 9½") rectangles (R10), 1 for each block.
• 60 (3⅛") squares (S9), 2 for each block.

From Fabric D (mint green), cut:
• 4 (6⅞" x 94") lengthwise strips for inner border.
• 5 (14") squares. Cut each square in quarters diagonally to get 18 quarter-square triangles for side set triangles (and 2 extra).
• 20 (9½") squares for alternate set squares.
• 2 (7¼") squares. Cut each square in half diagonally to get 4 half-square triangles (T6) for corner set triangles.

Making Blocks

1. For each block, select 1 rectangle and 1 T18 triangle. To mark centers, fold both pieces in half and lightly press a crease.

2. With right sides facing, match centers and raw edges. Start stitching about 1" from point of triangle and backtack. Sew a partial seam 2½" long, ending with another backtack *(Diagram A)*. Press seam allowance toward triangle.

3. Prepare 1 stem and 2 leaves for appliqué. Position stem on pieced unit, aligning tip of stem at top of triangle and base of stem with bottom edge of rectangle *(Diagram B)*. Appliqué sides of stem (top and bottom will be secured in seams). Position leaves as shown and appliqué. *(continued)*

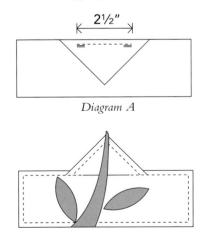

Diagram A

Diagram B

4. To piece diamonds and triangles, see instructions for sewing set-in seams (page 129). Make 3 of Unit 1 *(Diagram C)*.

5. To make and join remaining units, see instructions for making LeMoyne Star blocks (page 127). Make 2 of Unit 2. Join 1 Unit 2 to remaining Unit 1 as shown *(Diagram D)*.

6. Join Unit 2 to T18 triangle of base unit *(Diagram E)*.

7. Set-in remainder of block as for a star, sewing tip of stem in seam. When block is assembled, complete both sides of base seam *(Diagram F)*.

8. Repeat to make a total of 30 blocks.

Quilt Assembly

To assemble this quilt, set blocks on the diagonal, alternating with square set pieces. Set triangles fill in around the edge of the quilt.

1. Lay out blocks in diagonal rows, alternating blocks with set squares *(Quilt Assembly Diagram)*. Position a set triangle at end of each row as shown. Arrange blocks to get a pleasing balance of color and contrast.

2. Join blocks and set pieces in diagonal rows as shown. Press seam allowances toward set pieces.

3. Join rows.

Adding Borders

1. Mark the center of each Fabric D border strip.

2. See instructions on pages 20 and 21 for making a mitered corner. Measure quilt from top to bottom and side to side.

3. Measuring from center mark, measure length of quilt on 2 border strips. Mark corner end points. Pin borders to quilt sides, matching centers and corners, and stitch.

4. Measure and mark width of quilt on remaining 2 borders. Pin and sew borders to top and bottom edges of quilt. Press seam allowances toward borders.

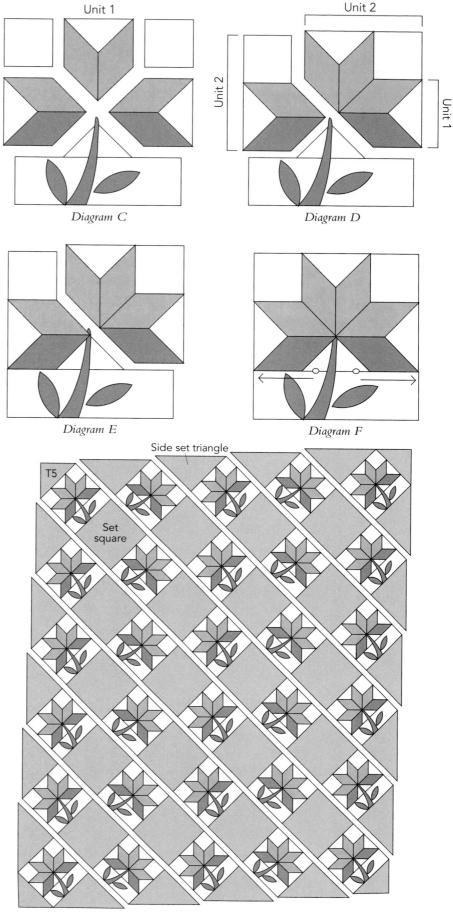

Diagram C

Diagram D

Diagram E

Diagram F

Quilt Assembly Diagram

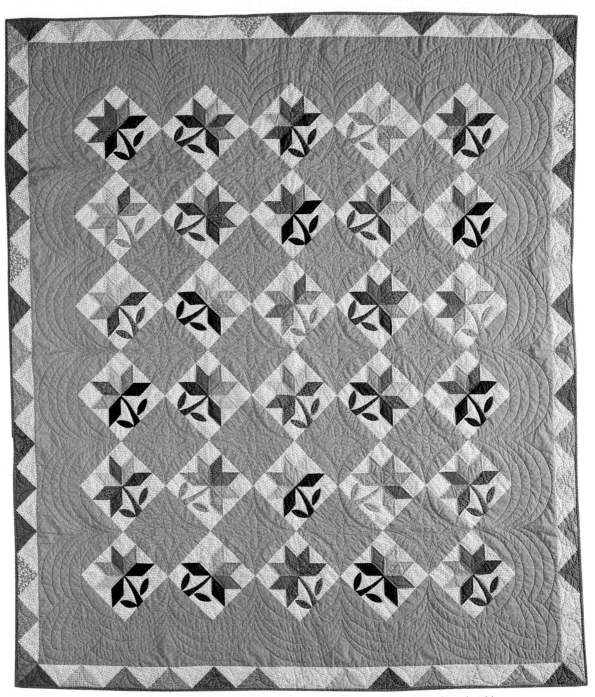

Peony by Joan Dawson, Bothell, Washington, 1995. Hand-quilted by
Joan Dawson and Lily Meyer. Quilt design by Marsha McCloskey.

5. Miter border corners.

6. Sort T15 triangles for dogtooth border. For each side row, select 13 Fabric A triangles and 14 Fabric C triangles. For top and bottom rows, select 11 Fabric A triangles and 12 Fabric C triangles for each row. Join triangles in each row *(Diagram G)*. You should have 8 Fabric A triangles left over.

7. Referring to photo, join pieced borders to quilt.

8. Join remaining Fabric A triangles in pairs to make 4 corner units *(Diagram H)*. Join corners to quilt.   *(continued)*

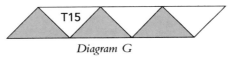

Diagram G

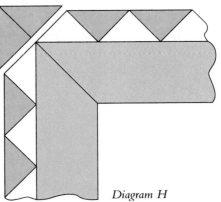

Diagram H

Finishing

1. Mark quilting design on quilt top as desired. Quilt shown has outline quilting in blocks and circles quilted around blocks into set squares and echoing into borders. Two other quilting suggestions are shown here *(Alternate Quilting Diagrams)*.

2. Divide the backing fabric into 3 (2½-yard) lengths. Cut 1 piece in half lengthwise and discard 1 half. Join wide panels to sides of narrow panel to assemble backing. Layer backing, batting, and quilt top. (Backing seams parallel top and bottom edges of quilt.) Baste. Quilt as marked or as desired.

3. Cut 10 yards of 1½"-wide bias binding. See page 26 for instructions on making and applying binding.

Alternate Quilting Diagrams

Size Variations

	Twin	King
Finished Size	57" x 95½"	95½" x 95½"
Number of Blocks	18	36
Blocks Set	3 x 6	6 x 6
Number of Set Squares	10	25
Number of Side Set Triangles	14	20
Number of T15 triangles		
Fabric A	48	60
Fabric C	44	56

Materials for Size Variations

		Twin	King
	Fabric A	1¼ yards	1¾ yards
	Fabric B	1 yard	1⅜ yards
	Fabric C	2 yards	3 yards
	Fabric D	3½ yards	5⅛ yards
	Binding fabric	⅝ yard	¾ yard
	Backing fabric	5⅞ yards	9 yards

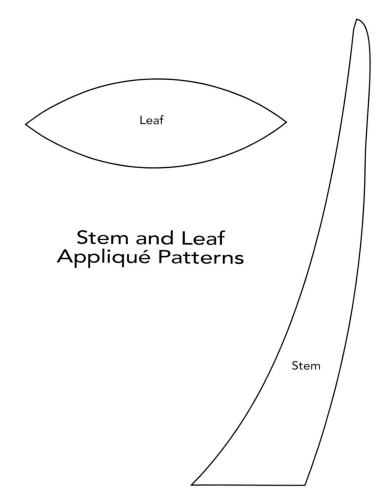

Leaf

Stem and Leaf Appliqué Patterns

Stem

Feathered Star Medallion

Feathered stars are not difficult to piece—they just have a lot of pieces. I choose a project like this when I have time to enjoy careful cutting and sewing. I allow about 10 hours to make the quilt top, using templates and cutting with scissors. Rotary cutting makes it a bit quicker. Large-scale prints, cut randomly, work well in this design.

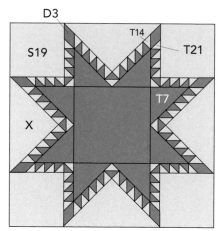

Feathered Star Block

Materials

▮	Fabric A (blue large floral print)	3¼ yards
▯	Fabric B (light small floral print)	2¼ yards
▯	Fabric C (blue plaid)	1¼ yards
	Binding fabric	¾ yard
	Backing fabric	4 yards
	Precut batting	72" x 90"

* This quilt fits a twin-size bed without a pillow tuck. To adapt this design for other sizes, adjust number and width of borders as desired.

Cutting

Instructions are for rotary cutting. To check cutting accuracy, compare rotary-cut pieces to patterns D3, S10, S16, S19, T7, T14, T15, and T21 (see pattern index, page 146). For traditional piecing, use these patterns to make templates.

From Fabric A (large floral), cut:
- 4 (10" x 72") lengthwise strips for outer border.
- 4 (13½") squares for bias-strip piecing.
- 1 (8½") square for star center. Cut this from a section of print that you like. (I prefer to choose an asymmetrical section rather than to center a large flower in the square.)
- 4 (7⅝") squares. Cut each square in quarters diagonally to get 16 quarter-square triangles (T15) for pieced border.
- 4 (4⅞") squares. Cut each square in half diagonally to get 8 half-square triangles (T7) for star block.
- 1 (1½" x 24") strip. With right sides facing, fold strip in half and cut 1⅝"-wide diagonal segments to get 4 D3 and 4 D3 reversed for star tips. See page 13 for tips on cutting rhomboids from strips.

From Fabric B (light small floral), cut:
- 4 (3¼" x 36") lengthwise strips for Border 2.
- 4 (13½") squares for bias-strip piecing.
- 1 (11¼") square. Cut square in quarters diagonally to get 4 quarter-square X triangles for star block.
- 3 (10⅝") squares. Cut each square in quarters diagonally to get 12 quarter-square Y triangles for pieced borders.
- 2 (10¼") squares. Cut each square in half diagonally to get 4 half-square Z triangles for pieced border corners.
- 4 (6⅛") squares (S19) for block corners.
- 20 (2") squares. Cut each square in half diagonally to get 40 half-square triangles (T14), 8 for star block and 32 for pieced border.
- 4 (1⅞") squares. Cut each square in half diagonally to get 8 half-square triangles (T21) for star block.

From Fabric C (blue plaid), cut:
- 8 (3¼" x 39") lengthwise strips for borders 1 and 3.

Bias-Strip Piecing Triangle-Squares

See page 16 for detailed instructions on bias-strip piecing two-triangle squares.

1. With right sides facing, match 1 (13½") square of Fabric A with a 13½" square of Fabric B.

2. Cutting through both layers, cut squares diagonally from corner to corner to establish true bias (45° angle). Measuring from cut edges, cut 8 sets of 2"-wide bias strips and 2 sets of corner triangles *(Diagram A)*.

3. Join each pair of bias strips; then join pairs to complete a bias-strip setup as shown *(Diagram B)*. Join corner triangles. Press all seams open.

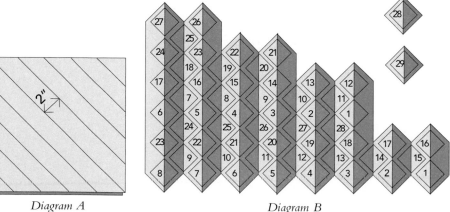

Diagram A   *Diagram B*

4. Using a square ruler with bias marking, rotary-cut 28 (1½") S16 triangle-squares for star block. Set aside remainder of this setup.

5. Use remaining 13½" squares to make 3 more bias-strip setups. From these (and remainder of first setup), cut 180 (1⅝") S10 triangle-squares, 36 for star block and 144 for pieced border (9 for each of 16 border units). You'll get 57 triangle-squares from each setup. *Note:* The difference between S10 and S16 squares is small, so it's easy to get them mixed up. I keep the squares separated in labeled envelopes or zip-top bags until I need them.

Making Block

In many feathered stars, partial seams enable us to avoid set-in seams. In the following diagrams, brackets indicate seams that are partially sewn early in construction of the block and completed later. Begin and end these seams with backtacking.

1. For 1 side unit, select 1 Triangle X, 9 S10 triangle-squares, 2 T7 triangles, and 2 T14 triangles.

2. Join 4 triangle-squares in a row, adding a T14 triangle to end of row as shown *(Diagram C)*. Join row to Triangle X with a partial seam as shown. Press seam allowances toward Triangle X.

3. Join remaining 5 triangle-squares in a row as shown, adding T14 to end of row *(Diagram C)*. Join row to Triangle X with a partial seam, stopping at last triangle-square as before.

4. Join T7 triangles as shown to complete unit *(Diagram D)*.

5. Repeat steps 1–4 to make a total of 4 side units.

6. For 1 corner unit, select 1 S19, 1 D3, 1 D3 reversed, 2 T21 triangles, and 7 S16 triangle-squares.

7. Sew T21 triangles to 1 shorter (bias) side of each D3 piece as shown *(Diagram E)*. One unit is a mirror-image of the other.

8. On D3 reversed unit, join 3 triangle-squares in a row as shown *(Diagram F)*. Join row to S19 square. Join 4 triangle-squares to remaining D3 unit as shown; then join row to S19 to complete unit.

9. Repeat steps 6–8 to make a total of 4 corner units.

10. Sew 2 side units to opposite edges of center square *(Block Assembly Diagram)*. Press seam allowances toward square. Join corner units to remaining side units, making 2 rows as shown. Press seam allowances toward corners.

11. Join rows. Then complete partial seams as shown. *(continued)*

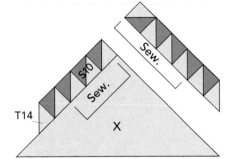

Diagram C

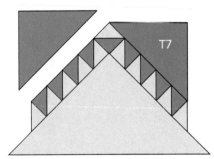

Diagram D

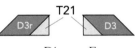

Diagram E

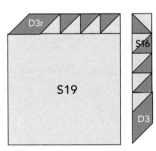

Diagram F

Sew remainder of partial seams last.

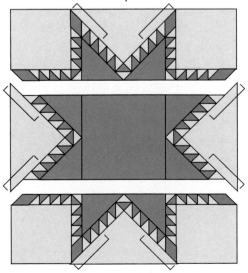

Block Assembly Diagram

Making Pineapple Border Units

1. For each border unit, select 9 S10 triangle-squares, 2 T14 triangles, and 1 T15 triangle.

2. Join 4 triangle-squares in a row, adding a T14 triangle to end of row as shown *(Diagram G)*. Join row to T15. Press seam allowance toward triangle.

3. Join remaining 5 triangle-squares in a row as shown, adding T14 to end of row *(Diagram G)*. Join row to other side of T15.

4. Repeat steps 1–3 to make a total of 16 pineapple units.

Adding Borders

1. Referring to instructions on page 20, measure star block from top to bottom; then trim 2 Fabric C border strips to match length. Join borders to block sides.

2. Measure block and borders from side to side; then trim 2 more Fabric C strips to match width. Join borders to top and bottom edges. Press seam allowances toward borders.

3. Join borders 2 and 3 in same manner.

4. For each side of pieced border, select 4 pineapple units and 3 Y triangles *(Pineapple Border Assembly Diagram)*. Press seam allowances toward Y triangles. Make 4 pieced borders.

5. Sew 1 pieced border to each side of quilt. Press seam allowances toward Border 3. To finish pieced border, sew Z triangles to corners *(Quilt Assembly Diagram)*.

6. Repeat steps 1 and 2 to join outer border strips to quilt.

Finishing

1. Mark quilting design on quilt top as desired. Quilt shown is outline-quilted, with a variety of heart and flower motifs quilted in open areas.

2. Divide backing into 2 (2-yard) pieces. Join lengths to assemble backing.

Layer backing, batting, and quilt top. Baste. Quilt as marked or as desired.

3. Cut 7½ yards of 1½"-wide bias binding. See page 26 for instructions on making and applying binding.

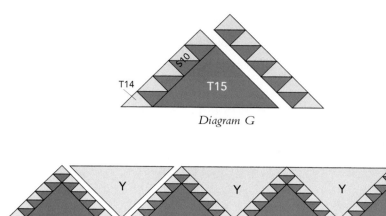

Diagram G

Pineapple Border Assembly Diagram

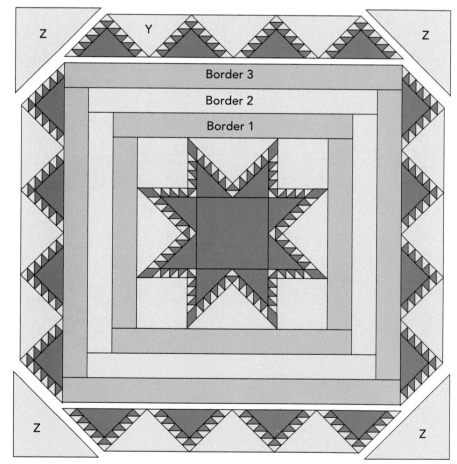

Quilt Assembly Diagram

Feathered Star Medallion by Marsha McCloskey, Seattle, Washington, 1995.
Machine-quilted by Barbara Ford.

Radiant Star

Of all feathered stars, I think the Radiant Star is the easiest to piece. It is also my favorite!

I made this quilt with scrap strips left over from other projects, but you can get

the same look if you cut bias strips from an assortment of fabrics to make triangle-squares.

Borders and lattice of a lush cabbage rose print frame the piecing with elegance.

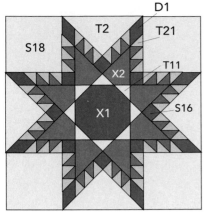

Radiant Star Block

Materials

■	Fabric A (assorted blue and rose prints)	1½ yards total
■	Fabric B (assorted navy prints)	½ yard total
■	Fabric C (assorted light prints and solids)	½ yard total
■	Fabric D (muslin)	1¾ yards
	Fabric E (large floral print)	2¼ yards
	Fabric F (dark rose print, including binding)	1¾ yards
	Backing fabric	4½ yards
	Precut batting	81" x 96"

This quilt fits a twin or full-size bed. For queen/king-size, make 16 blocks.

Cutting

Instructions are for rotary cutting. To check cutting accuracy, compare rotary-cut pieces to patterns D1, S16, S18, T2, T11, T21, X1, and X2 (see pattern index, page 146). For traditional piecing, use these patterns to make templates.

From Fabric A (blue and rose prints), cut:
• 13 (8") squares for bias-strip piecing.
• 36 (3⅜") squares. Cut each square in half diagonally to get 72 half-square triangles. From these, cut 72 kites (X2), 8 for each block. See page 12 for tips on cutting kites from triangles.

From Fabric B (navy prints), cut:
• 9 (4¾") squares. Use Cut-away Triangle below to trim corners from each square to make 9 octagons (X1), 1 for each block. See Cutting Corners, page 121, for details on this technique.
• 8 (1½" x 22") strips. From these, cut 72 (1½") D1 diamonds for star tips, 8 for each block. See page 12 for tips on cutting diamonds from strips.
• 88 (1½") squares (S16), 8 for each block and 1 for each cornerstone.

From Fabric C (light prints), cut:
• 10 (8") squares for bias-strip piecing.

From Fabric D (muslin), cut:
• 3 (8") squares for bias-strip piecing.
• 9 (7½") squares. Cut each square in quarters diagonally to get 36 quarter-square triangles (T2), 4 for each block.
• 36 (4⅞") squares (S18), 4 for each block.
• 36 (2⅛") squares. Cut each square in half diagonally to get 72 half-square triangles (T11), 8 for each block.
• 72 (1⅞") squares. Cut each square in half diagonally to get 144 half-square triangles (T21), 16 for each block.
• 64 (1½") squares (S16), 4 for each cornerstone.

From Fabric E (large floral), cut:
• 4 (6" x 76") lengthwise strips for outer borders.
• 24 (3½" x 15½") lengthwise strips for lattice.

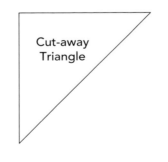

Cut-away Triangle

From Fabric F (dark rose print), cut:
• 4 (2½" x 63") lengthwise strips for inner borders.

Bias-Strip Piecing Triangle-Squares

See page 16 for detailed instructions on bias-strip piecing two-triangle squares.
1. With right sides facing, match 1 (8") square of Fabric A with an 8" square of Fabric C.
2. Cutting through both layers, cut squares diagonally from corner to corner to establish true bias (45° angle). Measuring from cut edges, cut 4 sets of 2"-wide strips and 2 sets of corner triangles (Diagram A). *(continued)*

2"

Diagram A

3. Join each pair of bias strips; then join pairs to complete a bias-strip setup as shown *(Diagram B)*. Join corner triangles. Press seams open.

4. Using a square ruler with bias marking, rotary-cut 19 (1½") S16 triangle-squares from this setup.

5. Repeat with remaining 8" squares of fabrics A, C, and D to make a total of 252 two-triangle squares, 32 for each block and 4 for each cornerstone.

Making Blocks

Sewing partial seams enables us to avoid set-in seams in this block. In the following diagrams, brackets indicate seams that are partially sewn early in construction of the block and completed later. Begin and end these seams with backtacking.

1. For center unit, sew a T11 triangle to each trimmed corner of X1 *(Diagram C)*. Press seam allowances away from X1.

2. For 1 side unit, select 1 T2, 1 T11, 2 T21, 4 triangle-squares, 2 X2, and 1 S16 of Fabric B.

3. Join 2 triangle-squares in a row, adding a T21 triangle to end of row

as shown *(Diagram D)*. Press seam allowances open. Join row to T2 with a partial seam. Press seam allowance toward T2.

4. Join 2 more triangle-squares in a row with S16 square as shown, adding a T21 to end of row *(Diagram D)*. Press seam allowances open. Join row to T2 with a partial seam as before.

5. Join an X2 piece to 1 side of unit as shown *(Diagram E)*. Press seam allowance toward X2.

6. Join T11 to remaining X2 piece. Press seam allowance toward X2. Join this to top edge to complete unit.

7. Repeat steps 2–6 to make a total of 4 side units.

8. For 1 corner unit, select 4 triangle-squares, 1 S18, 2 D1, 1 S16 of Fabric B, and 2 T21. Join 2 triangle-squares, 1 T21, and 1 D1 in a row. Press seam allowances open. Join row to 1 side of S18 as shown *(Diagram F)*. Press seam allowances open. Join remaining pieces in a row; then join row to adjacent side of square as shown. Repeat to make a total of 4 corner units.

9. Sew 2 side units to opposite edges of center square *(Block Assembly Diagram)*.

Join corner units to remaining side units, making 2 rows as shown.

10. Join rows. Complete partial seams.

Making Star Cornerstones

1. For each cornerstone star, select 4 triangle-squares, 1 S16 square of Fabric B, and 4 S16 squares of Fabric D.

2. Join units in 3 rows of 3 squares each *(Cornerstone Assembly Diagram)*. Press seam allowances away from triangle-squares.

3. Join rows to complete cornerstone.

4. Repeat to make a total of 16 cornerstone stars.

Quilt Assembly

1. For Lattice Row, join 3 lattice strips and 4 cornerstones. Press seam allowances toward lattice strips. Make 4 lattice rows.

2. For Block Row, join 3 blocks and 4 lattice strips as shown. Press seam allowances toward lattice strips. Make 3 block rows.

3. Referring to photo for placement, join rows. Press seam allowances toward lattice rows.

Diagram B

Diagram F

Diagram C

Diagram D

Diagram E

Sew remainder of partial seams last.

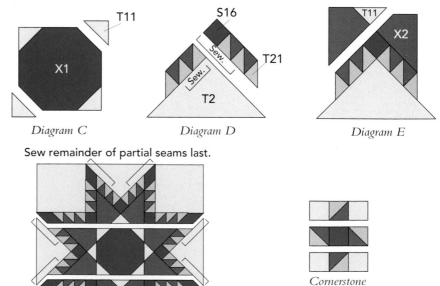

Block Assembly Diagram

Cornerstone Assembly Diagram

Radiant Star by Marsha McCloskey, Seattle, Washington, 1993.
Hand-quilted by Freda Smith.

Adding Borders

1. Referring to instructions on page 20, measure quilt from top to bottom; then trim 2 Fabric F border strips to match length. Join borders to quilt sides.

2. Measure quilt from side to side; then trim remaining Fabric F border strips to match width. Sew borders to top and bottom edges. Press seam allowances toward borders.

3. Join Fabric A border strips to quilt in same manner.

Finishing

1. Mark quilting design on quilt top as desired. Quilt shown is quilted in-the-ditch with outline quilting added in larger pieces and a simple cable in lattices. Borders are quilted with zigzag and clamshell designs.

2. Divide backing into 2 (2¼-yard) lengths. Join lengths to assemble backing. Layer backing, batting, and quilt top. Baste. Quilt as marked or as desired.

3. Cut 8½ yards of 1½"-wide bias binding. See page 26 for instructions on making and applying binding.

Rotary Cutting Charts & Pattern Index

Full-size patterns for the quilts in this book are on pages 148–157. Use these patterns to check the accuracy of rotary-cut pieces or to make templates for traditional cutting.

Solid outer lines are cutting lines, and dashed inner lines are seam lines. Finished sizes are printed in the seam allowances. The icon printed inside each piece shows the cut size, including seam allowances.

Some triangle patterns have two icons, indicating different grain directions (see cutting instructions for each project). Trim lines appear on patterns for those triangles and diamonds that require trimming for easy matching (see page 13).

Use squares with a diagonal line through the center to cut triangle-squares; the line corresponds with the seam line of a bias-strip setup.

Use the following charts to identify the page location of each pattern. These charts also tell you how to rotary-cut each piece from a 42" crosswise strip.

Squares

Pattern Number	Page Number	Width of Cut Strips	Width of Cross Cut	Squares per 42" Strip
S1	148	1⁹⁄₁₆"	1⁹⁄₁₆"	26
S2	148	1¾"	1¾"	24
S3	148	2"	2"	21
S4	148	3½"	3½"	12
S5	148	4¾"	4¾"	8
S6	148	6"	6"	7
S7	148	7½"	7½"	5
S8	149	1⅞"	1⅞"	30
S9	149	3⅛"	3⅛"	13
S10	149	1⅝"	1⅝"	25
S11	149	2⅝"	2⅝"	16
S12	149	3"	3"	14
S13	149	4"	4"	10
S14	149	5"	5"	8
S15	149	6½"	6½"	6
S16	150	1½"	1½"	28
S17	150	3¼"	3¼"	12
S18	150	4⅞"	4⅞"	8
S19	150	6⅛"	6⅛"	6
S20	150	2½"	2½"	16
S21	151	4¼"	4¼"	9

Diamonds*, Rhomboids* & Other Shapes

Pattern Number	Page Number	Width of Cut Strips	Width of Cross Cut	Pieces per 42" Strip
D1	157	1½"	1½"	17
D2	157	3"	4⅛"	6
D3	157	1½"	1⅝"	17
D4	157	2⅜"	2⅜"	11
D5	157	2⅝"	2⅝"	10
D6	157	4⅜"	4⅜"	7
X1	156	4¾"	4¾"	8
X2	156	3⅞"	3⅞"	20

Cut all diamonds and rhomboids at a 45° angle, except for D6. For D6, follow cutting instructions given for project.

Triangles

Pattern Number	Page Number	Width of Cut Strips	Width of Cross Cut	Second Cut*	Triangles per 42" Strip
T1	150	4"	4"	X	40
T2	150	7½"	7½"	X	20
T3	150	2⅜"	2⅜"	/	34
T3	150	3⅜"	3⅜"	X	48
T4	151	4¾"	4¾"	X	32
T5	151	5⅛"	5⅛"	/	16
T5	151	7¼"	7¼"	X	20
T6	151	7¼"	7¼"	/	10
T7	151	4⅞"	4⅞"	/	16
T8	151	2⅝"	2⅝"	/	32
T9	151	3"	3"	/	28
T9	151	4¼"	4¼"	X	36
T10	151	3⅜"	3⅜"	/	24
T11	151	2⅛"	2⅛"	/	38
T12	152	2¼"	2¼"	/	36
T13	152	5⅞"	5⅞"	/	14
T14	152	2"	2"	/	42
T15	152	7⅝"	7⅝"	X	20
T16	152	4"	4"	/	20
T17	152	6¼"	6¼"	X	24
T18	152	5"	5"	X	32
T19	153	3⅞"	3⅞"	/	20
T19	153	5½"	5½"	X	28
T20	153	6⅞"	6⅞"	/	12
T21	153	1⅞"	1⅞"	/	44
T22	153	1¹⁵⁄₁₆"	1¹⁵⁄₁₆"	/	42
T23	153	9¼"	9¼"	X	16
T24	153	2⅞"	2⅞"	/	28
T25	153	2¹³⁄₁₆"	5⁹⁄₁₆"	/	14

* / = cut in half diagonally; X = cut in quarters diagonally.

Rectangles

Pattern Number	Page Number	Width of Cut Strips	Width of Cross Cut	Rectangles per 42" Strip
R1	154	1½"	2½"	16
R2	154	1½"	3½"	12
R3	154	1½"	4½"	9
R4	154	1½"	5½"	7
R5	154	1½"	6½"	6
R6	154	1½"	7½"	5
R7	155	1½"	8½"	4
R8	154	2"	3½"	12
R9	154	1¾"	4¼"	9
R10	155	3⅛"	9½"	4
R11	155	2½"	6½"	6
R12	155	4¼"	9¼"	4
R13	156	2⅜"	5½"	7
R14	156	1½"	4¼"	9
R15	156	1¾"	3"	14
R16	156	1¾"	5½"	7

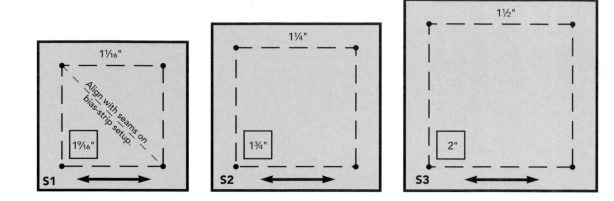

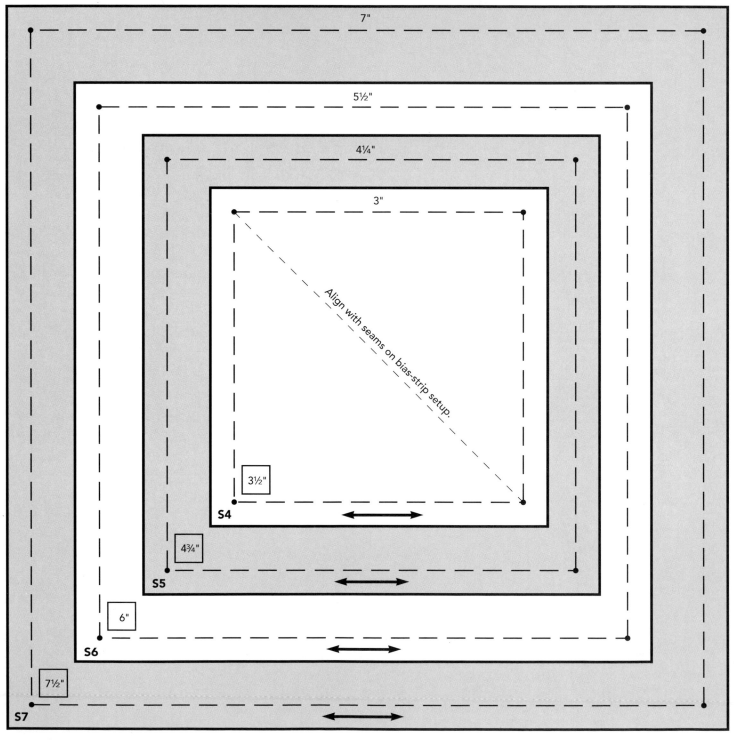

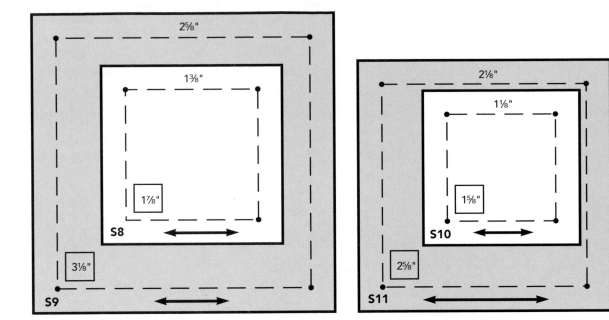

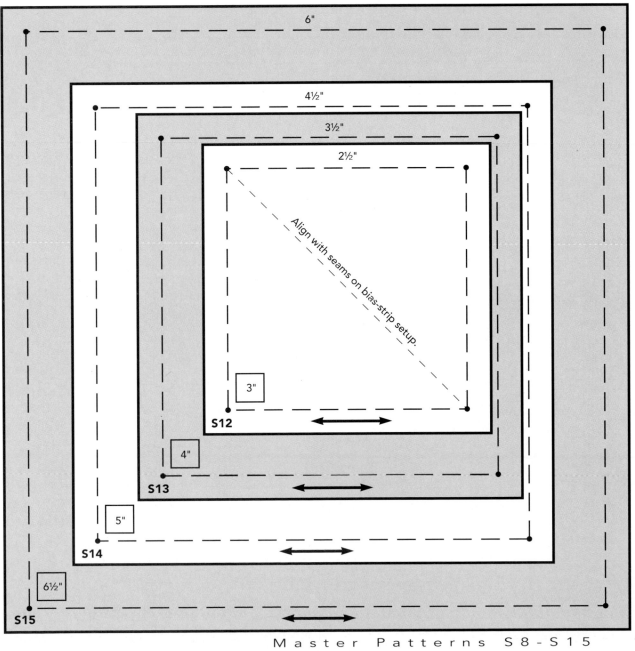

2⅝"

1⅜"

1⅞"

S8

3⅛"

S9

2⅛"

1⅛"

1⅝"

S10

2⅝"

S11

6"

4½"

3½"

2½"

Align with seams on bias-strip setup.

3"

S12

4"

S13

5"

S14

6½"

S15

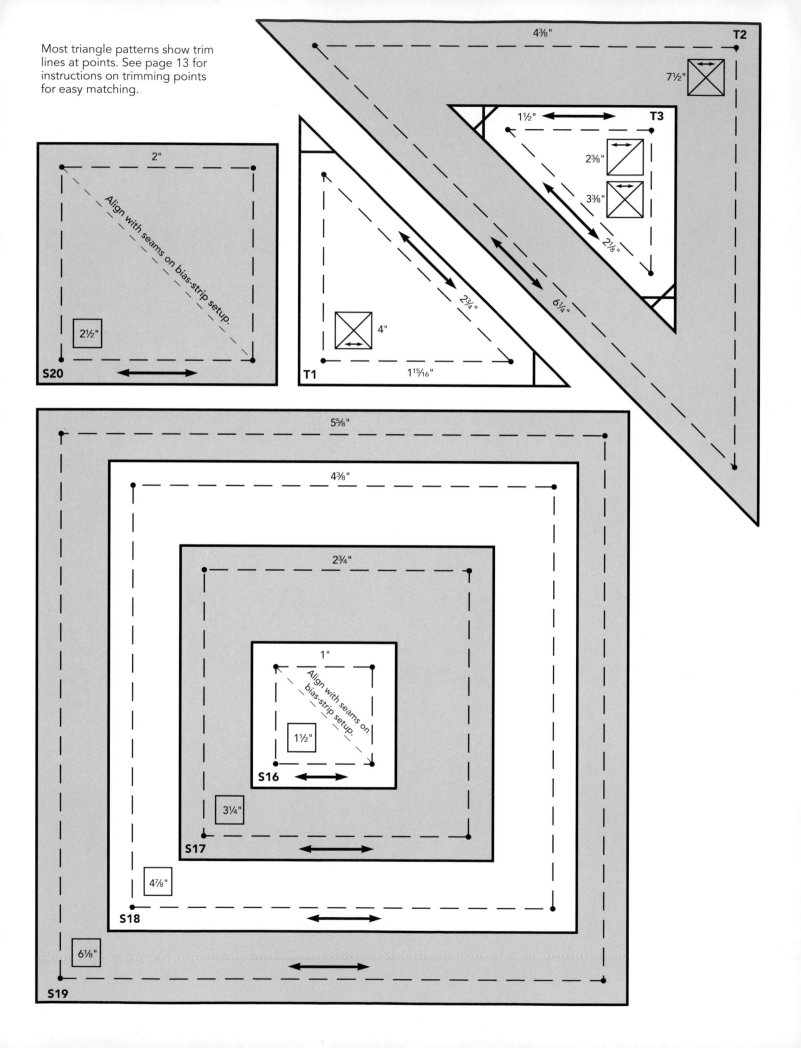

Most triangle patterns show trim lines at points. See page 13 for instructions on trimming points for easy matching.

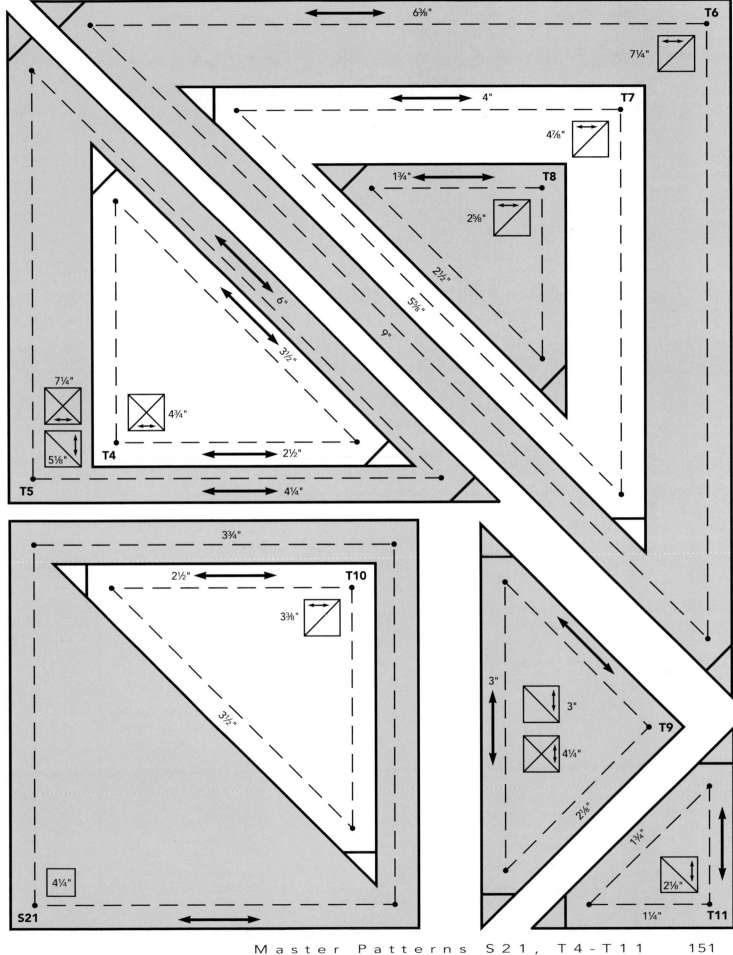

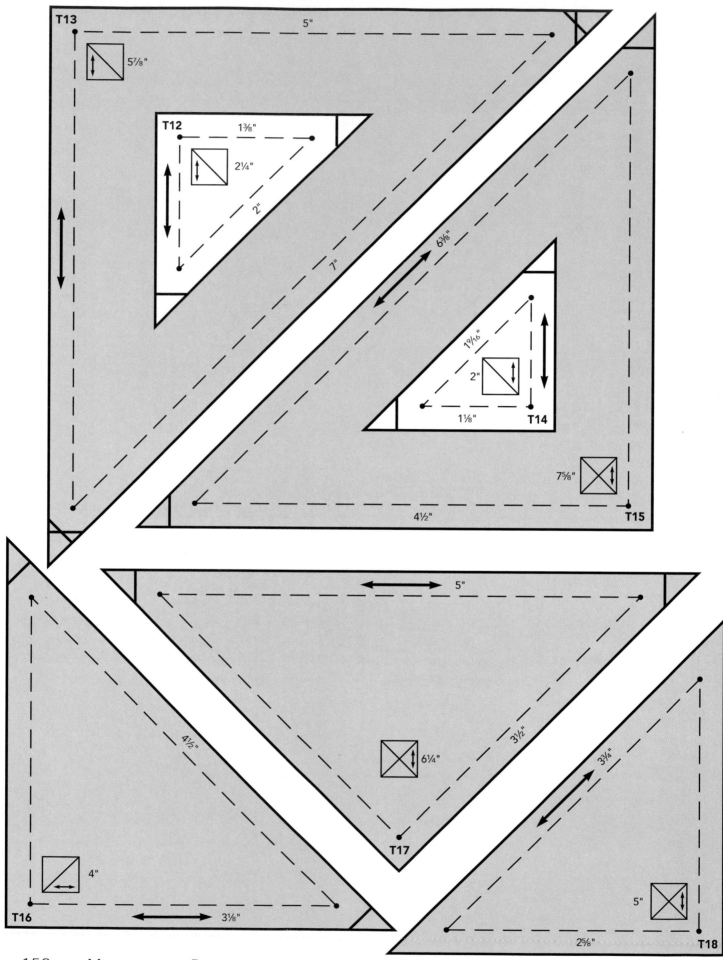

T13

5"

5⅞"

T12   1⅜"

2¼"

2"

7"

6⅜"

1⁹⁄₁₆"

2"

T14

1⅛"

7⅝"

4½"

T15

5"

4½"

3½"

6¼"

3¾"

T17

4"

T16   3⅛"

5"

2⅝"

T18

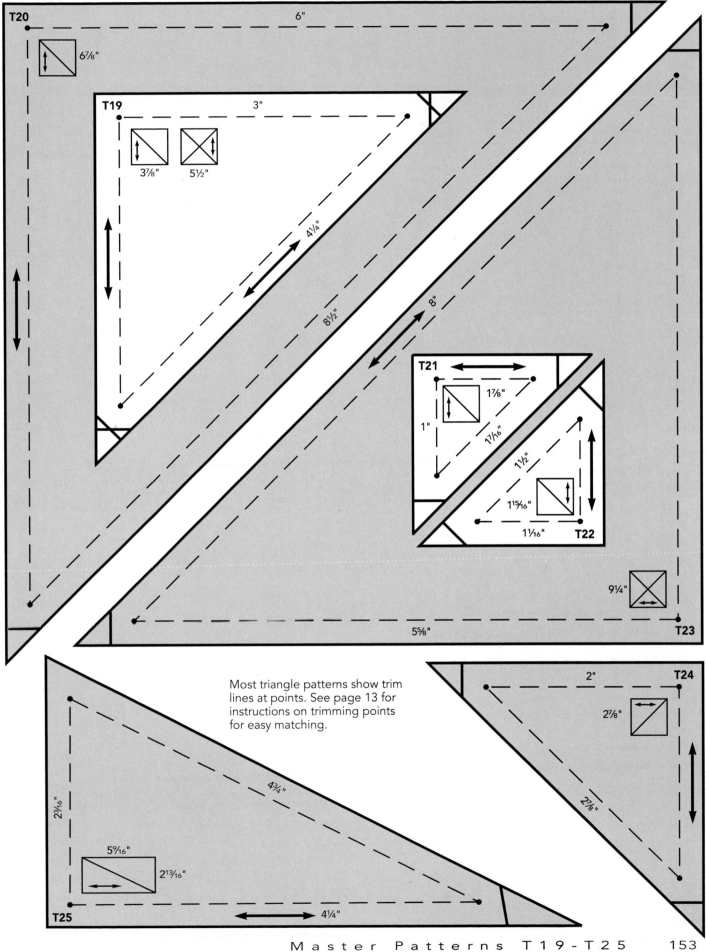

T20
6"
6⅞"

T19
3"
3⅞"   5½"
4¼"
8½"

8"

T21
1⅞"
1"
1⁷⁄₁₆"
1½"
1¹⁵⁄₁₆"
1¹⁄₁₆"
T22

9¼"
5⅝"
T23

Most triangle patterns show trim lines at points. See page 13 for instructions on trimming points for easy matching.

T24
2"
2⅞"
2⅞"

2³⁄₁₆"
4¾"
5⁹⁄₁₆"
2¹³⁄₁₆"
4¼"
T25

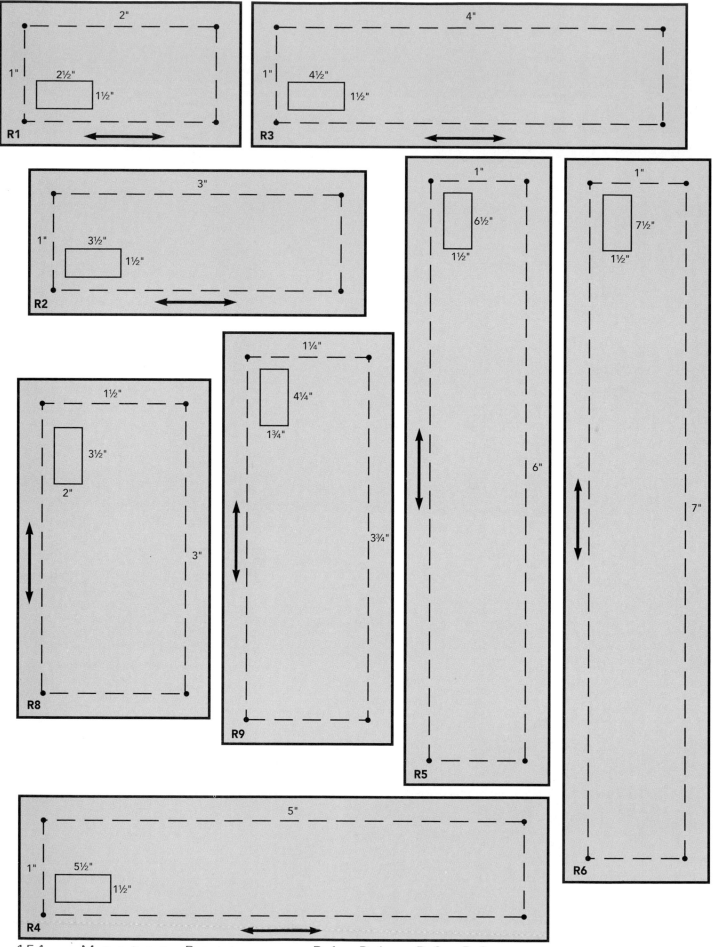

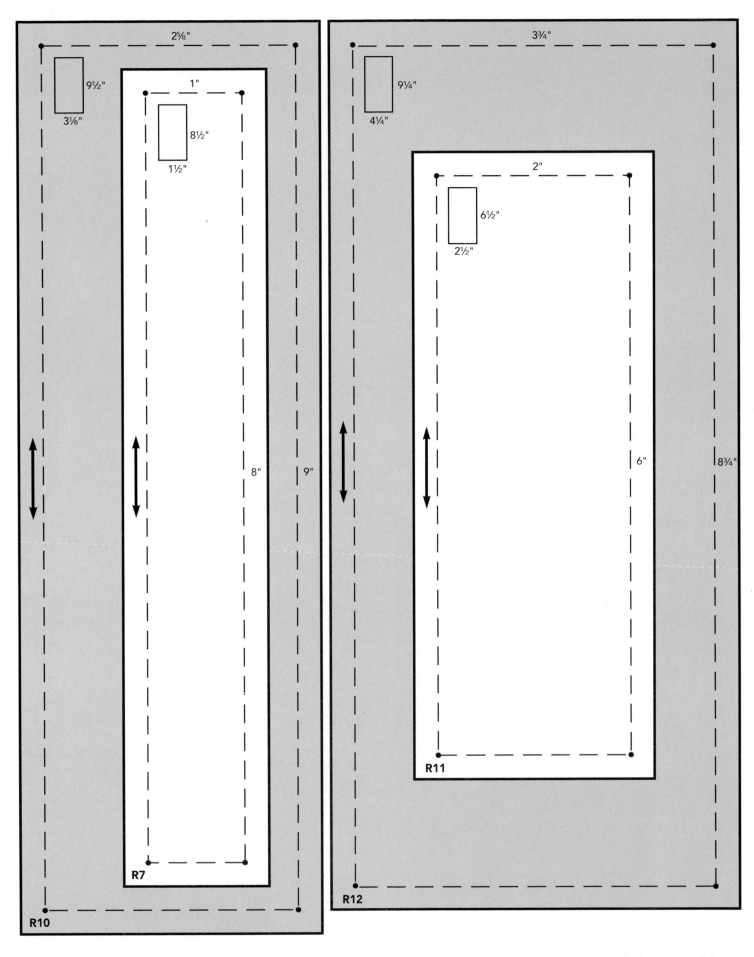

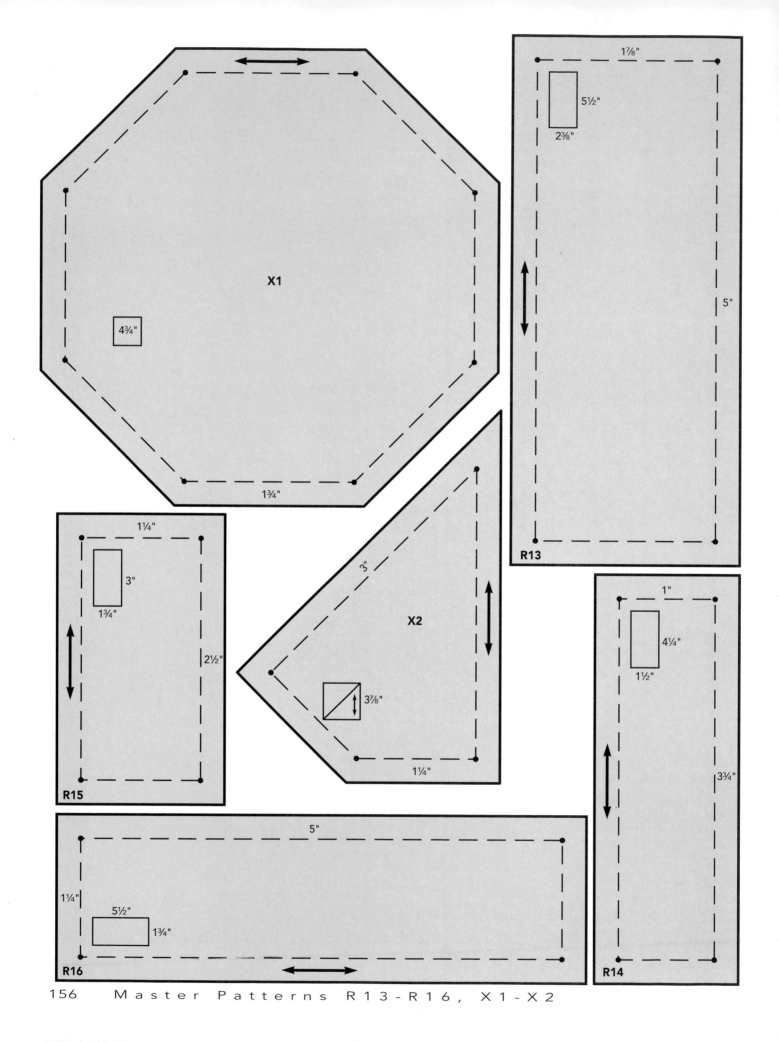

X1

4¾"

1¾"

1⅞"

5½"

2⅜"

5"

R13

1¼"

3"

1¾"

2½"

R15

3"

X2

3⅞"

1¼"

1"

4¼"

1½"

3¾"

5"

1¼"

5½"

1¾"

R16

R14

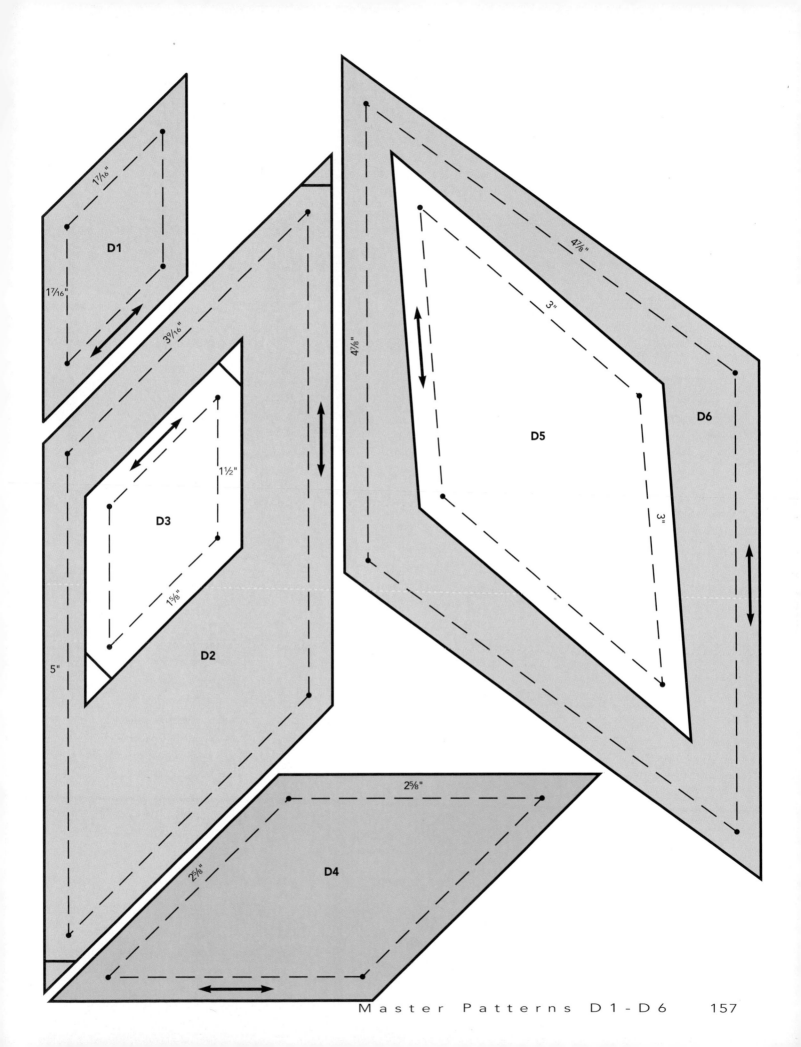

D1

1⁷⁄₁₆"

1⁷⁄₁₆"

3⁹⁄₁₆"

D3

1½"

1⁵⁄₈"

D2

5"

D4

2⁵⁄₈"

2⁵⁄₈"

D5

4⁷⁄₈"

4⁷⁄₈"

3"

3"

D6

Glossary of Terms

Alternate blocks. Two blocks that alternate across a row. Or unpieced fabric squares placed between blocks in a quilt set.

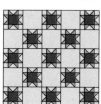

Appliqué. The process of sewing fabric pieces onto a larger background fabric, creating a layered, pictorial design.

Backing. The fabric that is the bottom layer, or back, of a quilt.

Backtack. Backstitching over a few stitches at the start or end of a seam. Used in patchwork for set-in seams and at mitered corners.

Basting. Lines of large, temporary stitches that hold the layers of a quilt together for quilting.

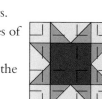
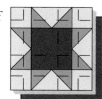

Batting. A soft filling between the patchwork top and the quilt backing.

Bearding. Migration of loose batting fibers through the quilt top or backing.

Between. A short, small-eyed needle used for quilting. Available in several sizes, indicated by numbers; the higher the number, the shorter the needle.

Bias. The diagonal of a woven fabric, which runs at a 45° angle to the selvage. This is the direction that has the most stretch, making bias ideal for curving appliqué shapes and for binding curved edges.

Bias-strip piecing. A quick-piecing method for making triangle-squares. See page 16.

Binding. A strip of fabric sewn around the edge of a quilt that covers the raw edges of the quilt.

Block. A repeated unit of a quilt design.

Borders. Pieced or plain fabric strips around the outside edge of the pieced quilt top.

Chain piecing. Machine sewing in

which units are sewn one after another without lifting the presser foot or cutting thread between units. Also called assembly-line piecing. See page 14.

Cornerstones. Squares that connect lattice strips at the corners of quilt blocks (sometimes called sashing squares).

Crosswise grain. Horizontal threads of a woven fabric, which run perpendicular to the selvage.

Cut dimension. Size of a patch before sewing, including seam allowance.

Cut-away triangle. A paper template, taped to the underside of a cutting ruler, which is used in rotary cutting to trim corners from fabric triangles or squares to create trapezoids or octagons. See page 121.

Cutting rulers. Rulers for rotary cutting are ⅛" thick transparent acrylic plastic, available in a variety of sizes and markings.

Design wall. A wall covered with flannel or cork on which components of a quilt can be pinned or hung for viewing.

Drawing rulers. A thin ruler, used for drawing. My favorite is 2" x 18" long printed with a red grid of ⅛" squares. Thicker rotary-cutting rulers are not good for drawing because they throw a shadow on the paper where the line is to be drawn.

Edge-to-edge stitching. In piecing, when lines of stitching extend from one raw edge of the fabric to the opposite raw edge.

Fat eighth. A 9" x 22" cut of fabric rather than a standard ⅛ yard (4½" x 45").

Fat quarter. An 18" x 22" cut of fabric rather than a standard ¼ yard (9" x 45").

Finished dimension. The size of a patch or a block after all sides are sewn.

Flying geese. Units made of a large triangle with two smaller ones sewn to the shorter legs.

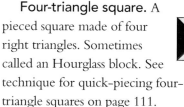

Four-Patch. A block comprising four squares or units, joined in two rows of two squares each.

Four-triangle square. A pieced square made of four right triangles. Sometimes called an Hourglass block. See technique for quick-piecing four-triangle squares on page 111.

Half-square triangle. The right triangle that results when a fabric square is cut in half diagonally. These triangles are straight grain on the short legs and bias on the hypotenuse.

Hanging sleeve. A fabric casing on the back of a quilt through which a dowel or curtain rod is inserted to hang the quilt on a wall. See page 27.

In-the-ditch. Quilting stitches worked very close to or in the seam line.

Kite. A symmetrical shape with four angles, which most often appears as points of feathered stars.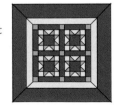

Lattice. Strips of fabric placed between quilt blocks. Sometimes called sashing.

Lengthwise grain. The vertical threads of a woven fabric, which run parallel to the selvage.

Match points. The point or corner where two seams meet.

Nesting. When seam allowances of matching seams fall in opposite directions, so that they fit into one another.

Nine-Patch. A block made of nine squares or units, joined in three rows of three squares each.

Outline quilting. A single line of quilting that parallels a seam line, approximately ¼" away.

Pin matching. Using straight pins to align two seams so that they will meet precisely when a seam is stitched.

Quarter-square triangle. The right triangle that results when a fabric square is cut in quarters diagonally, in an X. These triangles are bias on the short legs and straight grain on the hypotenuse. Set triangles on the outside of a diagonal set are cut in this manner to keep the outer edge on the straight grain.

Quick piecing. One of several techniques that eliminate some marking and cutting steps.

Quilt top. The upper layer of a quilt sandwich. Quilting designs are marked and stitched on the top.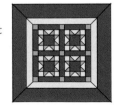

Quilting hoop. A portable wooden frame, round or oval, used to hold portions of a quilt taut for quilting. A quilting hoop is deeper than an embroidery hoop to accommodate the thickness of the quilt layers.

Quilting stitch. The sewing that holds the three layers (top, batting, and backing) of a quilt together.

Quilting thread. Thread that is slightly heavier than sewing thread and is specially designed to prevent snarling.

Repeat. A design unit within a pieced border that is duplicated continuously to create a design.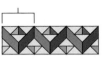

Reversed patch. A patchwork piece that is a mirror image of another. To cut a reversed patch, turn the template over (reverse it), or rotary-cut through two layers of fabric with right sides facing.

Rotary cutter. A tool, resembling a pizza cutter, with a very sharp blade. Used to cut fabric.

Sawtooth. A border treatment, made of two-triangle squares, that creates a jagged image. For examples, see photos of *Prairie Queen, Indiana Puzzle,* and *Cleo's Basket.*

Selvage. The woven edges of fabric as it comes off the bolt. More tightly woven than the body of the fabric, selvage is not used for sewing because it shrinks differently when washed.

Set (Setting). The arrangement of blocks and set pieces to make the overall quilt design. See page 18.

Set pieces. Elements of a quilt top that separate blocks, such as alternate blocks, lattice, or cornerstones.

Set-in seam. When three seams come together in a Y angle, one piece is set into the two that create the opening. These seams are stitched only to the seam line (match points), not edge to edge, and backtacked. See page 129.

Spacer strip. A plain border placed between the patchwork center and a pieced border to help with fit.

Stay-stitching. A line of machine stitching ⅛" from the edge of a fabric piece to prevent stretching.

Straight grain. The horizontal and vertical threads of a woven fabric.

Straight-strip piecing. A quick-piecing method for making squares and rectangles, particularly well-suited for piecing Four-Patch and Nine-Patch blocks.

Strata. In strip piecing, units made by joining two or more straight-grain or bias strips. Sometimes called strip sets. Strata are cut into small segments, which are then joined with others to form a design.

Strip set. A combination of strips that is cut into smaller segments that become units of patchwork.

Template. A duplicate of a printed pattern, made of sturdy material, that is traced to mark the shape of a quilt patch onto fabric.

Triangle-square. A patchwork square that is made of two or four triangles. (See two-triangle square and four-triangle square.) Triangles should be cut and sewn so that the straight grain falls on the outside edge of the square.

Two-triangle square. A pieced square made of two right triangles. See technique for bias-strip piecing two-triangle squares on page 16.

Value. The relative lightness or darkness of a color.

Marsha's Acknowledgments

My heartfelt thanks to the following:

♥ Quiltmakers Annette Anderson, Carole Collins, Reynola Pakusich, and Judy Pollard for their creativity and willingness to share their quilts.

♥ Monday Night Bowlers Joan Dawson, Cleo Nollette, and Terri Shinn, who turned my quilt drawings into reality.

♥ Quilter Freda Smith and two Midwest quilting services.

♥ Barbara Ford, whose good nature and magical machine quilting saved my time and my sanity.

♥ David Peha at Fabric Sales Company for supplying fabrics from my *Staples* line, shown on back cover and pages 1, 6–7, and 28–29.

♥ My daughter, Amanda—we worked together on the very first quilt and she helps me still.

Photography Credits
All photographs by **John O'Hagan** except the following:

Keith Harrelson: pages 1, 29, 30, 33, 38, 42, 46, 49, 54, 60, 67, 68, 72, 76, 80, 84, 105, 114, 119, 142.

Brit Huckaby: page 132.

Mail-Order Resources

Quiltmaking supplies are available at many craft and fabric stores, especially quilting specialty shops. Consult your local telephone directory to find a shop in your area.

If you prefer to have things delivered to your door, you can order supplies from a mail-order source. The following are good suppliers of fabric, batting, notions, and other quilting supplies. An ★ indicates companies that are mail-order sources for Marsha's fabrics.

Keepsake Quilting★
P.O. Box 1618
Centre Harbor, NH 03226
(800) 865-9458

Connecting Threads
P.O. Box 8940
Vancouver, WA 98668-8940
(800) 574-6454

In The Beginning★
8201 Lake City Way N.E.
Seattle, WA 98115
(206) 523-1121